THE GLOUCESTER BOOK OF DAYS

JILL EVANS

Thanks are due to the many authors and historians who have shared their knowledge and interests over the years, publishing their findings in books, magazines and journals, and, in the modern age, on the internet. Particular thanks are offered to those dedicated people who have taken on the daunting task of compiling indexes to the newspapers which have been published in Gloucester since 1722, in particular the *Gloucester Journal* and *The Citizen*. Without the efforts of all those people, the compilation of this volume would not have been possible.

The Julian calendar, which started the New Year on 25 March, was in use until the end of 1752. In this volume, the year is given as it was at the time of the event.

First published 2013

The History Press
The Mill, Brimscombe Port
Stroud, Gloucestershire, GL5 2QG
www.thehistorypress.co.uk

British Library Cataloguing in Publication Data.
A catalogue record for this book is available from the British Library.

ISBN 978 0 7524 6516 6

Typesetting and origination by The History Press
Printed in India

JANUARY 1ST

1903: Members of the Gloucester Orpheus Society gave their fifth annual concert at Shire Hall. The Society – a male-voice choir – had been founded by Herbert Brewer, the Cathedral organist, in 1898. A large audience attended to listen to a programme, which was later judged to be one of the best and most enjoyable yet provided by the Society. Members provided ten items to the programme, including Mr Lee, who contributed a song entitled *Encouragement to a Lover*. The composer listened to its performance from the body of the hall, and on its completion was compelled to take a bow. The President, Sir Hubert Parry, and the Conductor, Herbert Brewer, had both written pieces especially for the Society. Parry came onto the stage to conduct his own work, entitled *The Loyal Ode*. (*The Citizen*)

———— •◆• ————

1859: Gloucester folk who had made New Year's resolutions to get their painful feet seen to were informed in an advertisement that Mr J. Anderson would be available on January 7th and 8th only, at No. 9 Southgate Street, to treat 'tender feet'. Corns, bunions, 'callosities' and defective toenails could all be extracted in two minutes, using a new system, without cutting or causing the least pain. Mr Anderson's rates were 5 shillings per corn. (*Gloucester Journal*)

JANUARY 2ND

1888: At the City Petty Sessions, held on this day at the Police Courts in Gloucester, Mr Chipp, the Deputy Chief Constable of Police, was able to inform the Mayor that at this, the first court of the New Year, there were no prisoners to be tried and no summonses to be issued. Therefore, according to custom, he took great pleasure in presenting the Mayor with a pair of white kid gloves. He thought it spoke well for the citizens of Gloucester, which contained 32 miles of streets and nearly 40,000 inhabitants, that during the holidays no crime had been committed and no extension of opening hours in the inns abused. (*The Citizen*)

———— • ◆ • ————

1935: At a meeting of Gloucester City Council, it was decided to give the go-ahead to the building of the first municipal flats in Gloucester, on a new housing estate at Tredworth. There were to be 174 homes in total, consisting of 150 houses and twenty-four flats. It was expected that the cost of laying out the site would be about £7,904. The erection of the flats was strongly objected to by Councillors Blackwell and Edwards. Mr Edwards said flats were not desirable as habitations, and the only reason they were built in places such as London and Chicago was lack of land, which was not a problem in Gloucester. (*Cheltenham Chronicle*)

JANUARY 3RD

1887: *The Citizen* commented on the weather so far in the New Year as being 'old-fashioned' and 'seasonable'. There had been an intense frost on the night of January 1st, and the next day the canal was frozen, so skating was 'extensively indulged in'. (*The Citizen*)

1906: The inmates of Gloucester Workhouse were entertained by pupils of Barton House School. Dramatic scenes enacted included the trial scene from *Alice in Wonderland* and 'Mrs Gamp and Mrs Prig at tea'. There were also recitals and songs. The entertainment was quite different from the usual school display, but it was remarked that the performance gave evidence of a sound and thorough instruction in elocution, and the musical part of the programme was so good that the audience called for more. (*The Citizen*)

1942: It was reported that the Mayor of Gloucester, Trevor Wellington, had been made a Commander of the Order of the British Empire in the New Year's Honours List, for his work as Mayor and as ARP Controller for the city. Mr Wellington was in his fifth year as Mayor. Also honoured was Mr P.E.G. Sayer, Chief Test Pilot of Gloster Aircraft Company, who received an OBE. (*Gloucester Journal*)

JANUARY 4TH

1774: On this day, many of the citizens of Gloucester had gathered on the banks of the River Severn to enjoy the generosity of one of the parliamentary candidates for Gloucester, who had left 100 guineas with his agent, 'for the purpose of merriment'. The money had been used to provide a bullock, which was to be roasted whole, and two hogsheads of ale, for the public. As the river was frozen, it had been decided to roast the bullock on the ice. Once this had begun, the company, estimated at about 2,000, walked onto the frozen water to get their meal, but before they could get off again, the ice gave way and about 100 people went into the water. Unfortunately, about twenty of them were drowned. (*Gloucester Journal*)

1895: A meeting was held at Garrett's restaurant with a view to starting an Angling Society in Gloucester. Mr J. Thornbury took the chair, and the secretary and committee members were chosen. It was decided that the club should be called 'The Gloucester Popular Angling Association'. Subscriptions were to be 1s 6d a year, including the cost of a licence. (*The Citizen*)

JANUARY 5TH

1911: The annual County Ball was held at the Guildhall. The ballroom had been decorated in a pink and white colour scheme, with the walls hung with drapery and baskets of flowers suspended from festoons which linked the lights. The music was supplied by Herr Yantian's Austro-Hungarian Band, while refreshments were provided by John A. Fisher & Son, the well-known Royal Purveyors of Gloucester.

The stewards were Sir Lionel Darell, Sir William Guise, Colonel Curtis Hayward, Mr Michael G. Lloyd-Baker, Mr J.D. Crewdson and Mr W.F. Clifford. Over 300 guests were present and it was agreed afterwards that it had been a brilliant assembly, and successful in every way. (*Cheltenham Looker-on*)

January 6th

1889: A meeting of the Gloucestershire Engineering Society was held in the Co-operative Hall, to hear a lecture given by Professor Greenwood, on the subject of 'Steel'. Mr Platt (of Fielding and Platt) presided, and in introducing the lecturer, referred to steel as the material of the future for engineers, remarking that it was gradually superseding iron. Professor Greenwood then delivered his lecture, agreeing with the president as to the great future of steel. He described, at length, the different kinds of steel and the methods of manufacturing it, and at the close, answered questions from the audience. The lecturer was listened to with great attention by a large gathering of people connected with the engineering trade in Gloucester. (*The Citizen*)

JANUARY 7TH

1894: Conducting Sunday service at St Paul's Church, the Revd J. Talbot Gardiner said that before delivering his sermon, he wanted to make a few remarks concerning the disgraceful condition of the Cemetery Chapel. He had been conducting a funeral there on Friday, and when he entered the chapel he found several of the cemetery officials seated upon a bier in front of the fire, eating their dinner with their hats on. He did not blame the men, as it was very cold and they had to eat their meals somewhere. Besides, there was nothing to remind them that this was a consecrated building. It was dirtier and more cheerless than most people's kitchens, and there was not a single piece of church furniture or a Christian symbol to be seen. He blamed the members of the Gloucester Corporation, who 'distressed the feelings of the bereaved at a time when most were overcome with woe'. He wished to protest most emphatically against such a condition of things and hoped his hearers would help him in having it remedied. (*The Citizen*)

January 8th

1946: An ex-serviceman who was found in Gloucester to be in possession of a brass knuckleduster and a Colt .32 automatic pistol, loaded with two bullets, was sent to prison for six months by city magistrates. Bertram Ronald Langley, aged 26, of no fixed address, said he bought the firearm for £3 off an American who was broke, about a month previously. He said he carried the pistol because he had nowhere to keep it, being of no fixed address. He had tried to dispose of it with Gloucester and Cheltenham gunsmiths, and other people, including 'Yanks', without success. He carried the knuckleduster for self-defense, in case he stayed in a rough house and was attacked.

A charge that he was carrying the gun with intent to endanger life was dismissed, as there was no evidence of this. He was found guilty on three further charges; of being in possession of the pistol when he was not the holder of a firearms certificate, with being in unlawful possession of US Government property, and with stealing money from friends he stayed with in Bristol. He was sentenced to two months imprisonment for each offence, which were to run consecutively. (*Gloucester Journal*)

JANUARY 9TH

1806: Muffled bells were sounded from Gloucester's churches, to mark the funeral in London of 'the good, the great and immortal' Lord Nelson, who had been killed at the Battle of Trafalgar. (*Gloucester Journal*)

———◆———

1841: John Goulter Dowling, Master of the Crypt Grammar School, died. Born in Gloucester on April 18th 1805, the son of an alderman, he himself had been a pupil at the Crypt School. After taking his degree at Wadham College, Oxford, he was given the mastership of the Crypt School by the Corporation, who were the patrons of the establishment. He was ordained as a priest in 1829 by Christopher Bethell, the Bishop of Gloucester. In 1834, The Lord Chancellor presented him to the rectory of St Mary de Crypt Church, with St Owen's. He held this with the mastership of the school until his death. He was said to have been esteemed and greatly loved by his pupils, his parishioners and fellow citizens, who had a stained-glass window put into the great east window of his church, as a memorial. (*Oxford Dictionary of National Biography*)

JANUARY 10TH

1876: Albert Mansbridge, the founder of the Workers' Educational Association, was born in Gloucester. As the son of a carpenter, lack of money meant he had to leave school at the age of 14. He became a clerical worker, but continued to educate himself, and attended university extension courses at King's College, London. Eventually he began teaching courses himself, while still doing clerical work for a living. He felt that university extension courses were elitist, being aimed at the upper and middle classes. In 1903, he founded 'An Association to Promote the Higher Education of Working Men', a name wisely changed to the Workers' Educational Association (WEA). Mansbridge was able to leave his clerical job in 1905, becoming full-time General Secretary of the WEA. He died on August 22nd 1922, in Torquay. (*Encyclopedia Britannica*)

JANUARY 11TH

1817: A sentry who was on guard at the hospital of the 28th Regiment, near the Foreign Bridge, was attacked and gored by a cow which was being driven out of town. His body was ripped open from the groin upwards and his intestines badly injured. He was conveyed to the Infirmary without much hope for his recovery, but the skill and attention of the surgeon there meant he was expected to recover. (*Gloucester Journal*)

· ◆ ·

1878: At Gloucester Magistrates' Court, fourteen publicans were summonsed, charged with selling gin adulterated with water. In the case of Thomas Barnes of the Bell Inn, Barton Street, evidence was given by two police constables who had gone into the inn on September 25th the previous year, and bought half a pint of gin, which was sent for analysis. The sample was found to be 26 per cent gin and 74 per cent water. Barnes was fined ten shillings and costs, and his Counsel notified the court that he would appeal, because of irregularities in the way the gin sample was obtained. The other cases were left on file until the outcome of the appeal was known. In London the following month, Barnes's conviction was quashed. (*The Citizen*)

JANUARY 12TH

1886: A cab-driver named Thomas Overthrow was involved in an accident in Bristol Road. He was returning from taking a fare and had reached the Robinhood Inn, when his horse shied and bolted towards the Wagon Works. It had not gone far when it reached a coal cart and a timber wagon, and tried to pass between them. The cab was lifted off its wheels and the driver was thrown heavily to the ground. The horse dashed off again, but was caught before further damage was done. Overthrow was taken to the Infirmary, where he lay for two hours in a semi-conscious state. Fortunately, he had not suffered any serious injury, and was expected to be able to resume work before long. The horse and cab belonged to Mrs Franklin, of the Ram Mews. (*The Citizen*)

———◆◆———

1948: A small fire broke out at the home of the Cathedral organist, in College Green. It was found that the gas had been ignited by a short circuit of the electricity. (*Gloucester Journal*)

January 13th

1930: *The Citizen* reported that the level of the Severn was at a few inches over 20 feet. The waters had risen by 9 inches after two days of very heavy rain, and on this day the water was 2 inches over the quay wall. A big tide was expected in three days' time, which would cause the river to rise by as much as 12 feet. There was already some flooding, as the waters had not completely receded since the last time the river had burst its banks. The cricket pavilion on Castle Meadow, which had been floating about in the water since the last floods, had been secured to a tree, but during a gale the previous night, it had 'turned turtle', spilling out its contents – cricket bats and stumps – which were now floating around the meadow. (*The Citizen*)

JANUARY 14TH

1909: The High School for Girls' new building in Denmark Road was formally opened by Lord Stanley of Alderley. The school had first opened in 1883 as a Girl's Lower School, under the control of the Gloucester United Endowed Schools governing body. Its first home was at Mynd House in Barton Street, then in 1904 it moved to Bearland House. In 1906, the school was renamed the Girls' High School, and provided education for females aged between 8 and 18 years. Three years later, the school moved again, this time to a purpose-built building in Denmark Road, and became Denmark Road High School for Girls. Under the Education Act of 1944, it became a secondary grammar school. (*The Citizen; A History of the County of Gloucester, Volume IV: The City of Gloucester*, ed. N.M. Herbert, 1988)

JANUARY 15TH

1817: An auction was held at the Ram Inn, Gloucester, for a 'desirable Freehold Estate' belonging to Edward Tipton, a vintner, dealer and chapman, who had been declared bankrupt. As well as an estate in Herefordshire, Tipton owned The White Hart Inn, situated in Southgate Street, which was described as 'the greatest thoroughfare for travelling in the City of Gloucester'. It offered commodious stabling, excellent cellaring and attached and detached offices. According to the auctioneer's advertisement, the inn had been long celebrated as a travellers' house, as well as a place for conducting town business, and was 'too well known as such to require any recommendation through the medium of an advertisement'.

Also on offer was 'a desirable and commodious dwelling-house, conspicuous shop and premises', eligibly situated for trade in Westgate Street, almost opposite the new Shire Hall, occupied by Mr Whittick, perfumer, and another premises and shop adjoining, in College Street, then occupied by Mr William Smart. Those interested were invited to send for further particulars, by post-paid letter, to Messrs Bowyer, Mr W.C. Ward, or Mr Chadborn, Solicitors, of Gloucester. (*Gloucester Journal*)

JANUARY 16TH

1794: The idea of having a lunatic asylum in Gloucester had first been raised at a meeting of the Gloucester Infirmary Board in January 1792. In September 1793, it was resolved that a 'General Hospital for Insane Persons' should be established, and fundraising began. After four months, sufficient funds had been gathered to call a general meeting of subscribers, which took place on this day. At the meeting, a treasurer, secretary and committee were appointed, and a declaration was made that the Gloucester Lunatic Asylum was proposed to be 'a general establishment for the reception of all persons offered for admission who should be adjudged to be labouring under an unsound state of mind'.

Although there had been a good start to the raising of subscriptions, it took until 1811 for enough money to be collected for building work to begin, and it was another two years before a site was chosen in the parish of Wotton. Finally, in July 1823, the committee met to adopt the rules of the establishment, and the hospital was ready to accept its first patients. The asylum became known as the Horton Road Hospital. (Bailey, A., 'An Account of the First Gloucestershire County Asylum, now Horton Road Hospital, Gloucester, 1792-1823', in *Transactions of the Bristol and Gloucestershire Archaeological Society*, Volume 90)

JANUARY 17TH

1925: During a rugby match between Gloucester and the Old Blues at Kingsholm, forward Stanley Bayliss was injured after a line-out. He was taken to hospital in a critical condition and was found to have a damaged spinal cord. He died three days later. It was reported that he was conscious until shortly before his death. He was attended by his wife and parents, and fellow players Tom Voyce and Frank Ayliffe were also present.

At the coroner's inquest which followed, it was stated that Bayliss's injury was caused to the back of his neck as he ran with the ball after a line-out. He jerked his neck forward then fell down, with two forwards on top of him. In his evidence as a witness, the referee said there was a line-out and that Bayliss caught the ball and ran, was tackled, and then fell on his back. When admitted to the Infirmary, he was almost completely paralysed from the neck down. The Coroner found that there had been no foul play and a verdict of accidental death was returned.

Bayliss was 26 years old and was employed as a clerk by Western Farmers Ltd. He had played rugby for six years. In the First World War, he had served in the Royal Artillery. His funeral took place on January 23rd, with a service held at Northgate Wesleyan Chapel. (*The Citizen*)

January 18th

1804: A woman who was believed to have been abducted from her home in London was found safe and well at the Bell Inn, Gloucester. Mrs Lee, a famous beauty, was supposed to have been taken against her will by two brothers, Lockhart and Loudon Gordon. They had travelled from London into Oxfordshire, spending the night in Tetsworth, before continuing on their journey as far as Gloucester. Mrs Lee had shared a room at Tetsworth with Loudon Gordon, and the brothers found themselves standing trial at Oxford County Court, charged with abducting and 'defiling' her. They were acquitted, but the characters of both were commented on by the judge.

The Gordon brothers later published a pamphlet, giving their version of events. They said that Loudon had been in love with Mrs Lee and had asked her to elope with him. She agreed on condition that Lockhart, who was a clergyman, came with them, because Loudon was too young and not of high enough social position to protect her. When her servants saw her leaving with the brothers, Mrs Lee told them that she was going against her will, leading to a chase by a Bow Street Officer which ended at the Bell Inn. The Gordon brothers insisted that they had been victims of an artful and treacherous woman. (*The Times*)

JANUARY 19TH

1787: On this day, a 'wonderful large ox' owned by Anthony Mills, which had been touring the country and had appeared before the Royal Family twice, was shown at the New Inn. It was said to resemble an elephant in its hind parts, but was bigger. From nose to rump it measured 12 feet 10 inches. In girth, it was 12 feet 6 inches, and it was 18 hands and a half high. Despite its size, it was reported to be as tame and gentle as a lap dog. (*Gloucester Journal*)

———◆———

1941: Scouts and Guides from Gloucester, Cheltenham and Stroud attended a memorial service at the Cathedral, for the founder of the movement, Lord Baden Powell, who had died on January 8th. During the service, which was conducted by the Dean of Gloucester, the Scouts and Guides re-affirmed their promise to the movement. The Scouts were also mourning the death of Sir John Birchell, County Commissioner, who had done a great deal for Gloucestershire scouting. (*Gloucester Journal*)

JANUARY 20TH

1907: Christabel Pankhurst, co-founder with her mother Emmeline of the Women's Social and Political Union, visited Gloucester to speak about the Suffragette movement and the more militant tactics now being employed to gain publicity. Miss Pankhurst had been imprisoned in 1905 for shouting demands at a Liberal Party meeting. Her appearance at the Glevum Hall, at the invitation of the Gloucester branch of the Independent Labour Party, caused a great deal of excitement and the hall was packed, with some people not being able to gain admittance.

She received a warm reception when she rose to speak. During a long speech, she said forty-one women had been arrested so far during their campaign, and that she would like to see some Gloucester women prisoners – a comment that was greeted with nervous laughter. She said that the current campaign to give the vote to only a part of the female population would enfranchise an estimated one and a half million women, which would still be a very small portion of the electorate as a whole. (*The Citizen*)

January 21st

1899: A fire broke out at the premises of the Gloucester City and County Cycle Company Ltd, which was situated in Westgate Street, close to the Cathedral. The fire was spotted at about half past eight in the evening, in the back premises of the cycle depot. Shortly after the fire brigade arrived, the whole building was engulfed in flames. The various rooms were lined with pitch pine matchboards, which burned like tinder. The temperature was like a furnace, making it impossible for the firemen to reach the source of the blaze. After about an hour, the fire was suppressed, revealing hundreds of cycles lying in heaps on the blackened floor, their metal frames twisted into strange shapes. A shop on one side of the cycle shop had its roof largely destroyed. Boots the Chemist on the other side suffered no damage to its building, but much of its stock was spoilt by smoke and water. (*Western Daily Press*)

1921: A second High School for Girls was opened by the Gloucester United Schools governors, at Ribston Hall in Spa Road. Like the Denmark Road School, this establishment became a grammar school under the 1944 Education Act. In 1961, the school moved to new buildings in Stroud Road, but retained the name of their original site. (*A History of the County of Gloucester, Volume IV: The City of Gloucester*, ed. N.M. Herbert, 1988)

JANUARY 22ND

1795: Prince William, Duke of Gloucester, the brother of King George III, arrived in the city to take command of his regiment, which was quartered there. After spending the night at the King's Head, he reviewed his troops the next day, in College Green. Later, he treated his men to a dinner at the Booth Hall Inn. (*Gloucester Journal*)

1878: A meeting was held in the Tolsey to consider a scheme to establish a Coffee House Company in the city. Mr W.C. Lucy presided. The idea was to give people, especially working men, somewhere to go for refreshments which didn't sell alcoholic drinks. A coffee house had already been opened at the docks in 1877 and had been successful. A resolution was adopted in favour of forming a Gloucester Coffee House Company. The company opened its first coffee house in Eastgate Street, on May 25th 1878. (*The Citizen*)

JANUARY 23RD

1847: In its 'Nooks and Crannies of Old England' series, the *Illustrated London News* carried a sketch and piece on the old Booth Hall in Westgate Street. The timber-framed building was under threat of demolition, a new Shire Hall having been built next to it in 1816. The publication commented that Gloucester, like many other provincial towns, was rapidly losing its picturesque old timber houses, which were being replaced with new, modern buildings.

A building named the Booth Hall was believed to have been in use as a public meeting place, the Shire Hall and a market hall from at least 1559. The hall was accessed through an inn which fronted Westgate Street, and after the new Shire Hall was built, it was used as stabling for the hotel. Despite the fears expressed in the article, the Booth Hall survived for over 100 years more. The property became the Alhambra Music Hall in the 1860s, later renamed the Royal Albert Hall. In 1902, it was changed into the King's Theatre and Opera House which, from 1907, showed moving pictures as well as hosting live entertainments. It remained as an entertainment venue until the 1930s. During the Second World War, the hall was used as a storage depot. Finally, the old Booth Hall was demolished, to make way for an extension to Shire Hall, in 1957. (*Illustrated London News; A History of the County of Gloucester, Volume IV: The City of Gloucester*, ed. N.M. Herbert, 1988)

JANUARY 24TH

1820: The anniversary of the Gloucestershire Constitutional Whig Club was celebrated in Gloucester, on the birthday of the late Right Honourable Charles James Fox. It was raining heavily, and fears that the roads would become impassable prevented many of the members who lived in the countryside from attending, but a party of fifty gentlemen of the highest respectability still gathered. Colonel Berkeley was called to the Chair and presided. During the course of the morning, the club elected new officers. Colonel Berkeley was unanimously re-elected as President for the next three years, and M. Colchester Esq. was chosen as Vice-President. Several new members were then balloted for and enrolled.

At four o'clock the company sat down to an excellent dinner, served up by Mr Dowling in his best style. On the removal of the cloth, a great number of patriotic toasts were drunk and several speeches, 'fraught with sentiments of the most patriotic nature', were delivered with great effect. The party did not separate until a late hour. (*Bath Chronicle*)

January 25th

1616: William Laud, who had been installed as the Dean of Gloucester Cathedral by proxy the previous December, took his oaths in person at Gloucester and attended his first Chapter meeting on this day. Laud had been chosen by King James I to go to Gloucester and deal with the city's worrying puritan tendencies. The new Dean was soon causing tension at the Cathedral; one of his first acts was to move the communion table from the centre of the choir to the east end, much to the dismay of the Bishop of Gloucester, Miles Smith. It was said that Smith refused to enter the Cathedral again until Laud had gone.

Laud left Gloucester in 1621 to become Bishop of St David's. He became Archbishop of Canterbury in 1633. His High Church views and his closeness to King Charles I got him into trouble with the Long Parliament of 1640, which accused him of treason. He was imprisoned in the Tower of London in 1641 and executed on Tower Hill three years later. (Taylor, B., 'William Laud, Dean of Gloucester, 1616-21', in *Transactions of the Bristol and Gloucestershire Archaeological Society*, Volume 77)

JANUARY 26TH

1892: Gloucester Gymnasium Club members gave a display at the Public Baths in Barton Street. Hinton's band opened the proceedings by striking up a lively waltz, and twenty-eight members of the club trooped in, headed by the instructor, Mr Maxwell. The group went through dumb-bell practice, keeping time to the music. This was followed by six athletes performing on the parallel bars.

Sergeant-Major Hayward and Trooper Stokes next went through a sword exercise. Messrs Maxfield and Lugg then entered the arena with foils and fenced for about ten minutes. Mr Maxfield and six others then went through a performance on the vaulting horse, which was much enjoyed by the audience, as was the Indian club display given next. This was followed by a friendly boxing match, after which several members displayed their jumping abilities.

Sergeant-Major Bull was on next, to put twenty-four members through a physical drill, keeping time with the band. Sergeant-Major Hayward and Trooper Stokes then went through the lance exercise, after which there was another performance on the horizontal bars. Several members of the club, together with some boys from Sir Thomas Rich's School, showed off some somersaults next, after which there was another boxing bout. The entertainment was brought to a close by a tug-of-war. (*The Citizen*)

JANUARY 27TH

1884: On this Sunday morning, a fight took place at Robinswood Hill, between Henry Head and Henry Brown. Head, nicknamed 'Tails', and Brown fought for an hour and fifteen minutes, watched by about forty spectators. The fight ended when the police were seen approaching. The parties appeared in the Petty Sessions court on February 2nd. When asked if this had been a prize fight, Mr Chipp, the Deputy Chief Constable, replied that his information was that the fight was for one pound a side, but he believed it was really about rivalry as to who was the best fighter. Brown was said to have been the best man in Gloucester, and because Head and his friends were jealous, a fight was arranged. He believed 'Tails' had thrashed Brown, who appeared in court still badly bruised.

Both Head and Brown denied that the fight had been for money, and Brown said the two were now good friends. The chairman of the magistrates said prize-fighting had at one time been a popular pastime, patronised by gentlemen, but now it was only looked on as a barbarous sport. The defendants were bound over to keep the peace for twelve months. (*The Citizen*)

January 28th

1907: The inaugural meeting of a local branch of the Dickens Fellowship was held at Northgate Mansions. Mr H.W. Bruton presided. As well as about thirty gentlemen, a number of ladies attended. An apology for his inability to attend was received from Mr Henry Dickens, KC, from Egerton Place, London. The President said he was delighted to see the number of attendees, and that forty-nine people had joined the Fellowship so far. He welcomed Mr Yoxall, Honorary Secretary of the Birmingham branch.

Mr Yoxall congratulated them on their numbers, saying forty-nine members to start a branch was almost unprecedented. They should remember that they were not just members of their branch, but of the great Dickens Fellowship, which meant they formed part of the world-wide fellowship of members who were lovers and students of Charles Dickens and his works. The main aim of the Fellowship, in his opinion, was to spread a love of humanity, and a feature of the Gloucester branch should be friendliness and fellowship.

Mr Fox, at the request of the President, recited *The Cricket on the Hearth*, which was greatly appreciated. Light refreshments were then taken. It was decided that there should be six evening meetings and a summer meeting in the branch's first year. (*The Citizen*)

January 29th

1878: At Shire Hall, the Gloucester Temperance Society held a meeting, chaired by the Bishop of Gloucester. The event was crowded, many of the audience being made up of the local clergy and prominent supporters of the temperance movement in the city. The Bishop, Mr Ellicott, gave a lengthy speech concerning the evils of drink. He commented that a friend of his who was a local magistrate believed that alcohol was the cause of many of the crimes which he heard of when on the bench.

The Bishop made special mention of Samuel Bowley, a local merchant and Quaker, who was one of the founders of the local movement and who worked tirelessly in the cause. (*The Citizen*)

JANUARY 30TH

1860: A group of local merchants got together on this day to discuss the formation of a joint stock company to manufacture railway wagons. The meeting resolved to form the Gloucester Wagon Company, starting with capital of £100,000, with 10,000 shares being offered at a price of £10 each. In April the same year, the foundation stone of the Gloucester Wagon Works was laid on its site on the banks of the Gloucester & Berkeley Canal.

The company presented its first annual report in February 1861, which showed that the workforce had grown from 100 hands at the start to 360, and that 313 wagons had been turned out. In 1887, the company's name was changed to the Gloucester Railway Carriage and Wagon Company Limited. In January 1895, new buildings and a showroom were opened in Bristol Road. The company was taken over by Winget of Rochester in 1961, and from 1968 was known as Winget Gloucester. (www.glostransporthistory.visit.gloucestershire.co.uk)

1857: Gloucester's new cemetery was consecrated by the Bishop of Gloucester on a site at Tredworth. It was divided into two parts, with one side for Anglicans and the other for Non-Conformists. The building of a cemetery had become necessary after Acts of Parliament had been passed which prevented any more burials taking place in city churches and churchyards. (*Hereford Times*; *A History of the County of Gloucester, Volume IV: The City of Gloucester*, ed. N.M. Herbert, 1988)

JANUARY 31ST

1902: Deputy Chief Constable Nehemiah Philpott retired on this day, and attended his last police court in Gloucester. When he entered the courtroom, it was noticed that he was followed by two of his subordinate officers, who were each carrying a large basket containing tumblers. As it was known that there was to be a little ceremony to mark the DCC's retirement, it was hoped that 'something unusual in Police Court history' was going to happen. Unfortunately, those expecting to be invited to 'charge their glasses' were disappointed to discover that the items were an exhibit in the case of someone who was accused of stealing them. The Chairman of the Magistrates did say a few words, but no alcohol was imbibed.

In the evening, a supper was held for DCC Philpott at the Guildhall, hosted by the Mayor. Philpott was presented with a handsome gold, open-face, non-magnetic adjusted keyless English lever watch, with a massive 18-carat gold double Albert watch chain. On the watch was inscribed, 'Presented by the Magistrates of the City of Gloucester to Mr Nehemiah Philpott on his retiring from the office of Deputy-Chief Constable, after 46 years' service. 31st January 1902'. (*The Citizen*)

FEBRUARY 1ST

1690: Robert Frampton, Bishop of Gloucester, was deprived of the bishopric as a non-Juror. When William III and Mary became King and Queen of England in 1689, having deposed James II, all holders of benefices were required to swear an oath of allegiance to them. By Statute, anyone who did not do so was suspended from office on August 1st 1689, and was deprived on February 1st 1690.

Frampton was born in Dorset in 1622. He became Dean of Gloucester in 1673 and Bishop in 1681. He was by no means a pro-Catholic, having annoyed James II when he preached against Roman Catholicism at court. However, he believed James II ruled by divine right and no human had the power to remove him, so he refused to swear the oath of allegiance to William and Mary. In retirement, he officiated at the parish church at Standish and, on his death in May 1708, he was buried there. (*Oxford Dictionary of National Biography*)

February 2nd

1889: On this day, a Maori rugby team played a match against a Gloucestershire side at the Spa ground. The team from New Zealand had arrived at Plymouth in September 1888 and then travelled on to London on an Orient steamer. A tour involving nearly sixty matches, in England, Ireland and Wales, had been organised. The game at Gloucester took place on a bitterly cold day, before a crowd of between 7,000 and 10,000 spectators. The Maori side, described in the press as the 'dusky visitors', won the match. Two weeks later, the Maoris played an international against England. They set off on their journey back to New Zealand in March. (*The Citizen*)

———•———

1901: The funeral of Queen Victoria took place in London, and, in Gloucester, memorial services were held in all the churches. A Royal proclamation had been made that nationwide, all business was to be suspended on this day. In Gloucester, all of the markets closed, and the trams and buses didn't run. Flags in various parts of the city were flown at half-mast. Many of the prominent buildings, in particular the Guildhall and Shire Hall, were draped with material in the mourning colours of purple and black. (*The Citizen*)

February 3rd

1895: Due to a very harsh winter, made worse by flooding, many of the people in Gloucester were experiencing great distress. In response, the Mayor, Mr John Ward, had set up a fund for the relief of the poor. On this Sunday, the first soup kitchen organised by the fund was held in the Cattle Market; 400 loaves of bread and 400 quarts of soup were distributed. The distribution was organised by Mr T. Alger, who was helped by Mrs Alger, Mrs Watkins and Miss E. Coombs. During the morning, several ladies and gentlemen also visited the kitchen to help. There was no disorder and everything passed off satisfactorily. To make sure that the event did not turn into a scrum, tickets had been handed out to clergymen, ministers and others for distribution among needy people who had come to their notice. The soup kitchen was busy all morning and Mr Ager began making arrangements to hold another one on the following Sunday. (*The Citizen*)

FEBRUARY 4TH

1789: John Pitt won the parliamentary election in Gloucester, after a poll which had been kept open for fifteen days, the maximum legal length of time permitted. He won the contest by one vote. His opponent was the Whig candidate Henry Howard, believed to be a nephew of the Duke of Norfolk, who held great political power in the city. Pitt was a native of Gloucester, and his supporters declared that the freemen were determined to show that the city was not part and parcel of the Norfolk inheritance. The election commenced on January 19th. Pitt went well ahead at first, but Howard gained ground. The Tories brought in Gloucester freemen who were living in London, and the Whigs sought the help of the Duke of Norfolk, who was a Gloucester alderman. Finally, Pitt prevailed. On the following day, he was carried in a chair around the city. His Tory supporters formed a club, the 'True Blue Club', which met every year from then on to celebrate this famous victory. (*Gloucestershire Notes & Queries; The Times*)

February 5th

1876: *The Graphic* repeated a story from the *Livestock Journal*, of a valuable hen owned by a Gloucester boot-maker. Soon after this man became the owner, the hen laid one egg. The next day, she laid three; three days later she produced another eight, and in another week managed eleven in one day. (*The Graphic*)

———•◆•———

1906: *The Citizen* reported that a series of articles by Joseph Bennett had been appearing in the *Daily Telegraph* on the theme of 'Music in the Provinces', and that Gloucester was the subject of the latest piece. Bennett considered that if anything, the musical life of Gloucester was too full. There were so many societies practicing music and giving concerts that they somehow got in each other's way, and might be out of proportion to the number of concert-goers in the area. He gave particular mention to the Choral Society, the Orpheus Society, the County Orchestral Society, Mr E.C. Woodward's Orchestral Society, and the Co-operative Prize Choir. He believed that the Choral Society, particularly with Dr Brewer as conductor, was among the best in the kingdom.

Bennett wondered if the influence of the Three Choirs Festival had something to do with Gloucester's abundance of musical societies. He summed up by saying that music in Gloucester occupied a very distinguished position, of which both the city and county should be proud. (*The Citizen*)

February 6th

1802: Charles Wheatstone was born on this day at Barnwood House, Gloucester, the home of his grandparents. His father was a music-seller and flute teacher, with premises in Westgate Street. Charles was apprenticed to his uncle, a musical instrument-maker in the Strand, London. In 1823, his uncle died and Charles and his brother William inherited the business. In 1828, Wheatstone came up with his improvement of a German wind instrument, which became known as the English concertina, and was patented in 1829. Many other inventions were to follow, including the stereoscope and an encryption device called the Playfair cipher. He was a Fellow of the Royal Society from 1836, and he was knighted in 1868 for his contribution to the development of the telegraph. He died in 1875 and was buried at Kensal Green Cemetery in London. (*Oxford Dictionary of National Biography*)

———•◆•———

1895: At the City Petty Sessions, William Grenell was summonsed for assaulting Louisa Holland on February 1st. On that day, at dinner-time, she was going to work at Moreland's Match Factory, when the defendant threw a snowball at her, which struck her in the face. Osborne Scorgie, foreman at the factory, said the defendant was in company with about sixteen other youths who loitered about outside the factory and snowballed the girls as they came into work. Grenell said that he had aimed the snowball at his cousin, but he was fined and ordered to pay the costs. (*The Citizen*)

FEBRUARY 7TH

1885: A meeting was held at the Institute Hall in Southgate Street, to declare the free library connected with the Working Men's Institute open. The chairman, Mr F. Sessions, explained that the library had been in existence before, but they had to stop circulating the books owing to their dilapidated condition. Now, thanks to Mrs Robinson, who had kindly defrayed all the expenses connected with re-binding and mending the books, they were able to re-open the library. Mrs Robinson declared the library open, and Alderman Robinson made a few remarks on the value of good and instructive reading. (*The Citizen*)

FEBRUARY 8TH

1784: Gaol fever (a virulent form of typhoid) was raging at the County Prison in Gloucester Castle. Many of the prisoners were very ill and a number of them had died. The gaol-keeper, Mr Giles, was also very ill. On this day, the *Gloucester Journal* reported that a young man named Thomas Powell, the partner of an apothecary, who had been visiting the prison to tend to the sick, had also become a victim, having died of a malignant fever. (*Gloucester Journal*)

———— ◆ ————

1815: A numerous gathering of inhabitants of Gloucester took place at the Tolsey, to consider whether to send a petition to Parliament against the renewal of the Property Tax. The taxation had been brought in as a temporary measure, to finance the Napoleonic Wars, which ended in 1814, but the government had not abolished it by this time and it was feared that the tax would be continued in the next financial year. The meeting had just resolved to consider a draft of a petition when T. Davis Esq. rushed in and, after expressing regret that he had not been present when the resolution was put, moved an amendment that the petition should be rejected, which was seconded by Charles Church Esq., but upon a show of hands, only these two men supported the motion and it was agreed to send the petition. The Property Tax was not abolished until March 1816. (*Morning Post*)

FEBRUARY 9TH

1555: Bishop Hooper was burnt at the stake in St Mary's Square, between St Mary de Lode Church and St Mary's Gate, at the rear of the Cathedral. Hooper, who was a staunch protestant, had become Bishop of Gloucester during the reign of Edward VI. When Mary I succeeded her brother and restored Catholicism as the state religion, Hooper fell foul of the new regime. A false charge was drawn up against him, saying that he owed money to the Crown. He was in jail for a year, and when he refused to recant his Protestant beliefs, he was sent to Gloucester to be executed. The Bishop arrived in Gloucester on February 5th and is believed to have spent four nights in the house which is now part of the Folk Museum. (Brooks, R., *A Grim Almanac of Gloucestershire*, 2004)

———— •◆• ————

1626: On this day an agreement was drawn up between John Tilsley of Bristol and the Mayor and Burgesses of Gloucester, by which Tilsley was given a work base and loaned £200 to start up a pin-making business in the city. He was also supplied with about thirty boys to train as workers. By 1632 he had over fifty employees. By 1802 there were nine pin-making factories in Gloucester, employing 1,500 people. (*Gloucestershire Notes & Queries*; www.livinggloucester.co.uk)

FEBRUARY 10TH

1134: Robert Curthose died, and was subsequently buried in Gloucester Cathedral. He was the eldest son of William the Conqueror, born in about 1053. He rebelled against his father in 1077, instigating a feud which lasted for four years. When William died in 1087, Robert inherited the dukedom of Normandy, but his younger brother, William Rufus, was made King of England. Robert attempted to take England by force, but most of the Normans stayed loyal to his brother. When William Rufus died in 1100, Robert made a second invasion on England, but when he realised that the new king, Henry I, had strong support, he withdrew. In 1106, he was captured in Normandy and was imprisoned in the Tower of London until 1128, when he was transferred to Devizes and then moved on to Cardiff, where he died. (www.gloucesterhistory.co.uk)

FEBRUARY 11TH

1849: The Mariner's Chapel in the Docks was dedicated for public worship. It was intended that the chapel would provide for the spiritual needs of the sailors and boatmen who came to the port, and would be served by a chaplain who would be able to give them his undivided attention. The Revd James Hollins was appointed to be the chaplain, and he dedicated himself to his work with great enthusiasm. The seamen coming to the docks were of many different nationalities, and he organised services in foreign languages for them. He also went out to meet his flock, rather than waiting for them to come to him, making use of a portable organ which could be taken out to the quayside for open-air services. A Sunday school was organised for the children of boatmen, and religious tracts, written in many different languages, were distributed.

The chapel also held christenings, and the first one to take place there was on July 18th 1849, when Revd Hollins baptised James Partridge, the son of a carpenter from Sudbrook. (www. gloucestermariners.org.uk; Gloucestershire Archives, P154/23 IN 1/1)

FEBRUARY 12TH

1836: A notice bearing this date was printed in the *Gloucester Journal*, stating that the new Watch Committee, formed under the provisions of the Municipal Corporations Act, had put together a police force, which would begin operating on February 26th. The 'Constabulary Force and Police for preserving the Peace and protecting properties by day and night, and for apprehending offenders', was to be comprised of one Chief Constable, one Resident Sergeant (who would live at the Station House in Kimbrose Alley), two patrolling Sergeants, and twelve other Watch Constables of Police. Four of these constables would be on duty during the day, and eight at night. As well as these twelve, the four Sergeants of Mace and four Porters, in addition to their civic duties, were sworn in as constables. The four watchmen who were employed by the Gloucester & Berkeley Canal Company, besides being servants of the said company, were also sworn in as constables. Residents were warned that the new police would have jurisdiction in a seven mile radius of the city centre. (*Gloucester Journal*)

———— • ◆ • ————

1879: Thomas Hinds, a tramp, aged 59, appeared before Gloucester magistrates for begging in the streets. The case was adjourned until Friday, to give him the opportunity to leave the city. (*The Citizen*)

FEBRUARY 13TH

1882: An inquest was held in the Committee Room of the Infirmary, on the death of Richard Cornwall, aged 23, of Linton, near Ross, who died at the Infirmary during an operation. A house surgeon said the deceased had come to the outpatient ophthalmic department on November 2nd 1878, because his right eye had been injured in a dynamite explosion. He was admitted to a ward on February 11th, needing urgent surgery to have his right eye removed.

The operation took place the next morning. The house surgeon administered chloroform to the patient by pressing a towel over his face, in the presence of one of the ophthalmic surgeons. The operation had begun when the patient showed signs of reviving, so the towel was applied again, without additional chloroform being added. Straight away, his pulse began to weaken, so Nitrite of Amyl was applied to his nostrils, then artificial respiration was applied and continued for twenty minutes, but the patient did not revive. His heart had been examined before the operation and was fine. The post-mortem showed that all the organs were healthy. The verdict was that death was due to heart failure, owing to the administration of chloroform. (*The Citizen*)

FEBRUARY 14TH

1888: *The Citizen* commented that the increased popularity of sending Christmas, New Year and Easter cards had been met with a corresponding decline in the practice of sending Valentines cards on February 14th. The officials at Gloucester Post Office had been inconvenienced less than ever by it, which showed that the custom was dying out. As far as the Gloucester district was concerned, the sending of Valentines was more and more confined to 'the poorer classes', the missives being mostly 'cheap and nasty, consisting of long and highly coloured caricatures', which cost a penny. Those of 'the better class of people' who still clung to the practice tended to send Valentines of a more useful and handsome type. (*The Citizen*)

FEBRUARY 15TH

1903: The Assizes opened on Friday, February 13th, and on this Sunday, as was customary, the judge attended morning service at the Cathedral. This was a ceremonial occasion, and Mr Justice Jelf was conveyed from the Judges' Lodgings in Spa Road in the State Coach, attended by the County High Sheriff, the Sheriff's Chaplain, the City High Sheriff, the City Under-Sheriff, the Mayor and Corporation in state, and the sword and mace-bearers.

The judge was met at the West Door of the Cathedral by Archdeacon Hayward, various canons and minor canons and the Precentor. The procession went up the centre of the nave to the choir, accompanied by the National Anthem. The Bishop of Gloucester read the lesson, then the Sheriff's Chaplain gave a sermon. After, the Judge and the Corporation, headed by a long double file of police, processed out of the Cathedral, and the Judge went back in the coach to the lodgings. (*Gloucestershire Chronicle*)

February 16th

1915: A letter from the War Office was delivered to Mr and Mrs Cook of Gloucester, informing them that their son, Private George Cook of the 1st Battalion Gloucestershire Regiment, had been killed in action. Cook was a former Gloucester rugby player, who was playing for Oldham when the war started. About a week later, it was reported that Cook was not dead at all, as his parents had received a letter from him, saying that he had been a prisoner of war at Lille, and was currently in hospital being treated for a gunshot wound. (*Western Daily Press*)

1927: A performance of the comic opera *The Bandolero*, was given by the members of the St Mary de Lode Young Women's Recreation Club, at Priory Road Schools. The proceeds were in aid of St Mary's Home and the St Mary de Lode Poor Fund. There was a good attendance. Among the cast were Miss B. Crump, who played Manuel Alvarez, and Miss L. Ellis was Juanita. Miss N. Young took on the humorous role of Pepe (groom to Don Estaban), and Miss S. Newman gave a very creditable performance as Don Estaban. A further seventeen young women were in the cast. The accompanists were Miss D. McCain and Mr G.C. Cobb, and the entertainment was directed by Miss A.M. Clarke. (*The Citizen*)

February 17th

1893: An accident involving a trap occurred near Gloucester, which seriously injured a farmer's wife from Churcham. Mrs Imms had left the Fleece Inn in Westgate Street that evening, in a dog-cart driven by a waggoner's boy, aged about 13. At Over Bridge they met a hansom cab, and close behind this was Mr Burr's oil van. The boy drove past the cab, but then turned into the middle of the road and collided with the van. Both occupants of the cart were thrown out and Mrs Imms suffered a head injury.

Another cab which came upon the accident took Mrs Imms and the boy to the Infirmary, leaving behind the trap, which was badly damaged. She was admitted to a ward, but the boy appeared to be unharmed and he went in a cab to Churcham, to tell Mr Imms what had happened. Despite her injury, Mrs Imms was expected to recover. (*The Citizen*)

FEBRUARY 18TH

1929: The Theatre de Luxe in Northgate Street became the first cinema in Gloucestershire (and the fourth in the whole country) to show a talking picture. A journalist from the *Gloucester Journal* and *The Citizen* went to a private preview of Al Jonson in *The Singing Fool*, and was impressed with the sound quality, but did not think that the introduction of 'talkies' would mean the end of silent pictures. Comments supposedly made by locals were added to the advertisement for the film after the opening night, proclaiming, 'The greatest entertainment I've ever witnessed' and 'Would not have missed it for the world'. The Theatre de Luxe only survived for another ten years, being destroyed in a fire in January 1939. (Moore, A., *The Picture Palaces of Gloucester and Cheltenham*, 1989; *Gloucester Journal*)

FEBRUARY 19TH

1820: The centre of Gloucester was partially lit by gas for the first time. Crowds of spectators gathered in the city at nightfall to watch the lamps being turned on. On the first attempt, a quantity of atmospheric air in the pipes meant the lighting was dimmed, but at a later hour of night, the lamps shone brightly, making even distant objects almost as visible as they would be in daylight. At this time, new pipes were constantly being laid down. Although it was not intended that all the public lights would be powered by gas until September, individuals could be accommodated with as much gas lighting as they required in the meantime. (*Freeman's Journal*)

FEBRUARY 20TH

1904: This was a Saturday night, and two young men created a great commotion in the city centre. Francis Rowls from Swindon and his friend William Clarke from Gloucester, who were very drunk, were seen to go up the steps of the Albion Hotel, then come down again, pulling flowerpots off their stands as they went and kicking them in front of them. Clarke then put his fist through one of the hotel windows. In Southgate Street, the duo attracted the attention of a policeman, who later said in court that they were using the most obscene language he had ever heard in his life. Another policeman who came on the scene saw blood on Clarke's hand and asked him for his name and address, to which Rowls said, 'If you takes the one, you takes both'. Rowls went pretty quietly, but Clarke became violent and fell down, then kicked the constable twice as he put on the handcuffs. He had to be carried to the station, struggling all the way.

In court on the following Monday, both were sentenced to fourteen days in prison for the damage and for being drunk and disorderly. Clarke was given another month, with hard labour, for the assault on the policeman. (*The Citizen*)

FEBRUARY 21ST

1861: A violent storm with gale-force winds raged through Gloucester in the early hours of the morning. At about half past one, at the railway station, the fencing which separated the platform of the Great Western Railway terminus from that of the Midland Company began to sway, before a large part of it crashed to the ground. At the South Wales end of the platform, the corrugated iron portion of the roof was turned up as if it were made of paper. The roof of the Midland section was partly stripped, and throughout the station signal posts and telegraphic poles were blown horizontal. A nearby factory had its roof blown off, as did the Working Men's Institute. A chimney stack at Gillet's engine works was blown down, and the Cathedral also suffered some damage. Near the railway station, four magnificent elm trees were levelled, and in the whole Gloucester area, hundreds of elms, poplars and fruit trees were uprooted. Notwithstanding all the damage to property, there were no reports of injury to any people. (*Bristol Mercury*)

FEBRUARY 22ND

1737: A notice in the *Gloucester Journal* announced that at John Barnes's, 'at the Nait, near the Key, Gloucester', could be seen, or sold to the best bidder, a chair and four dogs, with a proper harness, 'able to carry a lusty man 20 Miles a Day'. Also to be seen at the same place were 'a Hairy Man and two Hairy Children'. A note was added that John Barnes made and sold all sorts of cat-gut strings, from the largest size to that of a fiddle string, and also 'Bakers and Butchers Horse Pots'. (*Gloucester Journal*)

———◆———

1901: A very successful Scottish dinner was held at the White Hart Hotel, Kingsholm, attended by over sixty Scots from Gloucester, Cheltenham and Hereford. The dinner was originally planned for Burns' Night, but the death of the Queen meant it was postponed. Mr James Muir presided, and in proposing the Loyal Toast he spoke of the late Queen's affection for Scotland and its people. The toast to 'the Memory of Burns' was drunk standing up and in silence. The Chairman suggested that a Caledonian Society should be formed in Gloucester, and the motion was carried unanimously. Before dinner, the haggis was brought in, accompanied by bagpipes played by Mr George Scott. The singing of *Auld Lang Syne* concluded a very jovial evening. (*The Citizen*)

FEBRUARY 23RD

1837: At the Gloucester Petty Sessions, Elizabeth Lane made a complaint against her husband, Charles Lane, for assaulting her. A summons was issued and Mr Lane appeared in court a few days later; the case was dismissed because the justices decided that the assault was justified. (Gloucestershire Archives, Gloucester Borough Records, GBR/G4/M1/1)

1944: A painting from Gloucester Cathedral, called the 'Last Judgement' or 'Doom', was destroyed in a bombing raid in London, at the studio where it had been sent to be restored. The work had been discovered in about 1800, behind some wainscoting in the nave, when seats were being removed for repairs. It was thought to be an altar piece from around 1540, which had been hidden shortly before the Dissolution. In 1934, on the advice of an art expert, it was sent to London for restoration. It was waiting for collection when the restorer's studio was destroyed. (Wallender, D., *The History, Art and Architecture of Gloucester Cathedral*, 1991)

FEBRUARY 24TH

1994: Gloucester police obtained a warrant to search the house and garden of No. 25 Cromwell Street, the home of Fred and Rosemary West. The search resulted in bodies being found, buried in the garden and in the cellar. Fred West was arrested on March 1st, and confessed to murdering nine females, including his daughter Heather, who had all been buried at Cromwell Street. He also admitted to killing his first wife Rena, his lover Anna McFall and his daughter Charmaine, all of whom were buried elsewhere. Rose West was arrested on April 25th. On December 13th, Fred West was charged on twelve counts of murder and was sent to await trial at Winson Green Prison in Birmingham. He hanged himself there on January 1st 1995. Rose West was then tried on her own for the murders. She was found guilty on ten counts of murder on November 22nd 1995, and was sentenced to life imprisonment. (*The Citizen*)

FEBRUARY 25TH

1942: A memorial service was held at All Saints' Church, Gloucester, for Lieutenant Michael J. Janvrin, younger son of Revd C.W. Janvrin, Rector of Withington and formerly vicar of All Saints. Lieutenant Janvrin, who was 23, had been second in command of the submarine *Triumph*, which the Admiralty had recently announced was overdue and must be considered lost.

The service was conducted by the vicar of All Saints, Revd W.E. Evans, and the lesson was read by the Bishop of Gloucester, Dr Headlam. Prayers were recited by the Bishop of Tewkesbury, the Rt Revd A.J. Hodson. A surpliced choir led the singing of hymns, which included *Fight the Good Fight* and *O Valiant Hearts*. Canon H. Maynard Smyth gave an address, saying they were there to commemorate Michael Janvrin and the ship's company of the *Triumph*. He felt that it was quite right that they should think of Michael in that church, for he had spent most of his boyhood in that parish and when he was at home he attended services at the church. It was twenty years since Canon Maynard Smyth first saw Michael, a rather shy little boy who did well at school and at Dartmouth. His career in the navy, though short, had been glorious. (*The Citizen*)

February 26th

1895: Alfred Wilkes, of No. 81 Barton Street, Tewkesbury, was brought before the magistrate at Gloucester police station, charged with stealing a pair of slippers. On the previous evening, Wilkes had gone into the shop of George Oliver in Westgate Street and bought a pair of patent leather boots for 5s 6d. After he left, it was discovered that the slippers were missing. Information was given to the police and from enquiries made, Sergeant Collett proceeded to the Theatre Royal, where he found Wilkes in the gallery. Wilkes refused to be searched and was taken to the police station, followed by a crowd of interested spectators.

In Berkeley Street, Collett saw the prisoner put his hand under his coat, then throw the slippers down and kick them into the crowd. They were retrieved by the shop manager and the prisoner said, 'Forgive me, don't have me locked up'. When charged at the station, he said, 'I have nothing to say; I had them'. In court, he pleaded guilty and was fined 28 shillings, including costs. The slippers were worth less than 2 shillings. (*The Citizen*)

February 27th

1546: Thomas Bell, a cap-manufacturer of Gloucester, was knighted on this day. Born in 1486, he had purchased Blackfriars after the Dissolution of the Monasteries, and turned it into a house called Bell's Place. The buildings in the grounds were used as a factory. Bell was Mayor of Gloucester in 1536, 1544 and 1553. He had the chapel of St Kineburgh converted into an almshouse for six poor people to live in. This became known as Kimbrose Hospital. Sir Thomas died on May 26th 1566, aged 80. A memorial to him was erected in the church of St Mary de Crypt. (www.livinggloucester.co.uk)

1902: A very successful social evening was organised by Messrs Hickman, Hudson and Wilton, held at Goddard's Assembly Rooms. About 150 guests attended and were treated to an excellent musical programme, after which 'dancing, parlour games, and ping-pong were indulged in'. The proceedings were enlivened by a string band, conducted by Mr Debenham. Votes of thanks were offered to the promoters and to Mr Pritchard, who acted as the MC, and to all who had made the meeting such a success. The evening closed with the singing of the National Anthem. (*The Citizen*)

FEBRUARY 28TH

1887: The Mayor presided over a rowdy meeting at the Corn Exchange, held to decide whether or not Gloucester should adopt the Free Libraries Act, which would mean the council would be able to put a charge on the rates to pay for the construction and maintenance of a public library. Mr W.C. Lucy moved a resolution in favour of the adoption of the Act. Mr W.P. Price and Mr C. Blackwell tried to speak in favour of the resolution, but were shouted down by opponents. Mr Trevor Powell spoke against it, not because he thought a free library was not desirable, but because he didn't think this was the right time, when men were out of work and business was slow. 'If the gentlemen who advocated it were so anxious to educate the citizens,' he said, 'let them put their hands in their pockets'. The resolution was put to the vote and a large majority voted against. The defeated side then demanded that a poll be held, which took place on March 7th. The result was 916 for the library, and 2,259 against. (*The Citizen*)

FEBRUARY 29TH

1904: A letter of complaint appeared in *The Citizen*. The writer wanted to draw attention to the amount of bad language that anyone proceeding through the streets of Gloucester at night was to hear. It was not fit for a lady to wend her way home, because she could not do this without hearing 'filthy language from the mouths of half-drunken hobble-de-hoys'. If the police would bring a case or two before the city magistrates, and make an example of them, it would soon stop this nuisance, or at least a good deal of it. The letter was signed, 'DISGUSTED'. (*The Citizen*)

1676: Edward Fowler was installed as a Prebend of Gloucester Cathedral on this day. Born in Westerleigh, he was educated at the College School in Gloucester. In 1680, promotion took him away from Gloucester, when he became vicar of St Giles, Cripplegate, in London. Five years later, he began writing against 'popery', which annoyed the king, James II. He regained Royal favour after James was deposed and replaced on the throne by William and Mary, and, in 1691, he replaced Robert Frampton as Bishop of Gloucester. He remained in the position until his death, on August 26th 1714. (*Oxford Dictionary of National Biography*)

MARCH 1ST

1902: At the County Petty Sessions in Gloucester, Leon Vint, who was well known at that time as the proprietor of 'Leon Vint's Globe Choir and Scenorama', was summonsed for a motoring offence. It was stated that he had allowed a motor car to be driven at a greater speed than 14 miles an hour, at Churchdown, on February 21st. PC Harding stated that he was on duty on the Cheltenham Road, near the Three Arches, when he saw the defendant and three other gents driving in a motor car coming from Gloucester and going in the direction of Cheltenham. The vehicle was being driven at between 20 and 30 miles an hour. The constable shouted to the defendant to stop, but he merely nodded at him and the car went on.

Vint did not appear in person, but wrote a letter to Deputy Chief Constable Harrison, stating that he was not the owner of the car, having sold it on the day of the incident to the man who was driving, and their speed had not exceeded 12 miles an hour. The Chairman said this was the first case of its kind they had heard, but it was so serious that it was their duty to impose the maximum penalty – £10 plus costs of 13s 6d. (*The Citizen*)

MARCH 2ND

1848: A race took place at Brockworth between two horses, an aged grey belonging to Mr Breen and a chestnut mare of Mr Blinkhorn, for a prize of 20 sovereigns. The chosen course was over three miles of 'good hunting country'. A large number of sporting gentlemen from Gloucester and Cheltenham came to watch. Mr Breen's horse took the lead at the start but fell at the fourth fence. Mr Blinkhorn's mare went ahead and won the race with ease. (*The Era*)

———◆———

1941: Pupils of Denmark Road Girls' High School entertained members of the Armed Forces, assembled at the YMCA canteen in Albion Street. The programme was a dramatic one, the first piece being an amusing sketch entitled *The Lost Property Office*. The final sketch, *Katherine Parr*, showed Henry VIII and his sixth wife at the breakfast table. Henry was played by Elizabeth Logan, Katherine by Daphne Russell, and the page by Jill Harris. The whole programme was produced under the direction of Miss Neve, the elocution and English mistress. Thanks were offered on behalf of the audience by Mr C.A. Bretherton, to the headmistress, Dr A.M. White, and everyone who had taken part. (*Gloucester Journal*)

MARCH 3RD

1673: John Dorney, former town clerk of Gloucester, was buried at the church of St Mary de Crypt. Dorney had played a prominent part in keeping the Royalists at bay during the siege of Gloucester, and was punished after the Restoration by being unseated from his position as town clerk in 1662. However, he was re-appointed to his former position in 1667. Dorney wrote an account of the siege of Gloucester, which was perhaps the most contemporary work on that subject, being published only seventeen days after the siege ended. (Austin, R., 'The City of Gloucester and the Regulation of the Corporations, 1662-3', in *Transactions of the Bristol & Gloucestershire Archaeological Society*, Volume 59)

MARCH 4TH

1907: For the second time in two days, Gloucester docks was the scene of a fire at a timberyard. The fire was discovered at about 7 o'clock in the evening, on the premises of Messrs Joseph Griggs and Co. Ltd, timber and slate importers. The yard, in Bristol Road, was next door to Messrs Nicks and Co., which had been the victim of the previous night's fire. The main area of the blaze was a large drying shed, containing a great deal of valuable timber.

Watched by a crowd of thousands, the fire engines of the Liverpool, London and Globe and the Norwich Union insurance companies attended straight away, and the Cheltenham and Stroud brigades were called in, as was the new fire float, the *Salamander*. This was the fire float's second outing in two days, having been acquired for the city in January. Its particular usefulness was that it was able to direct jets onto the building from the water, while the other engines worked from the road. The fire on this occasion was so fierce that it raged at full force for several hours, and the firemen had to work through the night to quench it completely. It was suspected that both incidents were arson, and this appeared to be confirmed the next day, when an attempt was made to fire the yard of Messrs Price, Walker and Company. (*The Citizen*)

MARCH 5TH

1787: Workmen at the Cathedral, who were taking up flat stones at the entrance of the choir, in order to repair the paving, found a stone coffin containing a well-preserved corpse. Remnants of a robe and of leather boots could be seen, and the body had in its hand a wooden crosier, decorated with silver gilt, and burnished. All of this plus other symbols in the coffin suggested that these were the remains of an abbot. After some historical research had been done, it was thought that this was Abbot Wigmore, who died on March 12th 1327. He was described as having been buried near the entrance of the choir, which he had built. This was not the first time that Abbot Wigmore's resting place had been disturbed. It had been discovered previously in 1741, when the screen behind the organ was erected by Bishop Benson. (*Gloucester Journal*)

MARCH 6TH

1624: Godfrey Goodman was consecrated Bishop of Gloucester. Bishop Goodman was to have an interesting career. He spent lavishly at Gloucester, and caused controversy by putting altar cloths with crucifixes embroidered on them in the Cathedral, an action which fuelled suspicion that the Anglican Bishop had leanings towards Roman Catholicism. In 1633, he was elected as Bishop of Hereford, but it was discovered that he had bribed officials to get the position, so he was forced to remain in Gloucester. In 1641, he was imprisoned by Parliament for having signed his adhesion to new canons which, among other things, upheld the divine right of kings. His imprisonment was rather harsh, as he had only signed the canons after being imprisoned for refusing to do so. After eighteen weeks, he was released on bail and ordered to return to his diocese. In 1643, the Bishop's Palace was sacked by parliamentary soldiers and he lost nearly all his papers and books. He left Gloucester, going first to his estate in Wales and then to London. He never returned to live in Gloucester, although he remained Bishop, dying in London in the mid-1650s. In his will, he stated that the Church of Rome was the Mother Church. (*Oxford Dictionary of National Biography*)

MARCH 7TH

1927: The Gloucester Liberal Association held a meeting, at which the question of Proportional Representation was debated. A resolution was unanimously passed, stating that the meeting recognised that Proportional Representation occupied a very prominent place in the Liberal Party's declared policy of electoral reform. It was suggested that at each opening of Parliament, if the subject was not mentioned in the King's Speech, then the Liberal members should table an amendment calling for 'immediate steps to be taken to secure more equitable representation of the country by means of electoral reform, on the lines of Proportional Representation'. The meeting also decided that copies of this Resolution should be sent to the Chairman of the Parliamentary Liberal Party and the Chief Whip of the Party, Sir P. Hutchinson, MP. (*The Citizen*)

MARCH 8TH

1122: A fire burnt in Gloucester while the monks in the Abbey of St Peter sang mass. The flames soon reached the abbey buildings, getting into the steeple. All of the minster was burnt down, and all of the treasures inside destroyed, apart from a few books and mass-vestments. (*Anglo-Saxon Chronicles*)

———•◆•———

1895: Henry Ryland, landlord of the Fountain Inn, Westgate Street, died suddenly. He was the son of another publican, Mr Ryland of the Welsh Harp in London Road. Henry Ryland had been in apparently good health, but on the morning of March 6th, while rolling up a blind, he was seized with a fit and fell heavily, sustaining a cut above the eye. He was put to bed and attended by Dr Brown and Mr Firmin Cuthbert, but he grew worse, became delirious, and finally died.

Ryland had succeeded Mr Cameron at the Fountain Inn, and was previously landlord of the East End Vaults. During the recent severe weather, Ryland, with Mr Furley, had distributed nearly 140 loaves of bread, together with soup, provided by subscription, to the needy poor three times a week. He left a widow, who was herself ill, and two little girls. (*The Citizen*)

MARCH 9TH

1888: The annual dinner of Gloucester Rowing Club was held at The Ram Hotel. Mr E.W. Coren presided and Mr John Fielding occupied the vice-chair. Also present was the City High Sheriff. After toasts had been drunk to the Queen and the Royal Family, Mr J.W. Coren, the Honorary Secretary, read the annual report. He stated that the crew representing the club at the various regattas had, unfortunately, been unsuccessful, but on land, they had achieved better results, having won the tug-of-war at the annual Gloucester Athletic Sports day.

The Chairman proposed a toast of 'Success to the Gloucester Rowing Club', and reminisced about his time as a rowing member in the club many years ago. He recalled that the members were not a very spirited lot, and never rowed in a match. He believed that rowing was one of the healthiest exercises that could be indulged in, and should be encouraged, even if prizes weren't won. (*The Citizen*)

MARCH 10TH

1538: This was the time of the Dissolution of the Monasteries, and on this day the Prior of Llanthony Secunda, Richard Hart, and nineteen of his canons signed a deed of surrender, handing over the priory to King Henry VIII. Llanthony was the first priory in England to be surrendered, according to the historian Atkyns. In return, the prior and all the canons were granted pensions.

In 1540, the prior's under-steward, Arthur Porter, bought the priory and 400 acres of its land, and used it as a farm. (Langston, J.N., 'Priors of Llanthony by Gloucester' in *Transactions of the Bristol and Gloucestershire Archaeological Society*, Volume 63; www.gloucester.gov.uk)

MARCH 11TH

1942: The funeral took place at St Mark's parish church, Gloucester, of Mr A.C. Rogers, who, for most of his professional life, worked for the same entertainment company. Born in London in 1865, Rogers came from very old theatrical stock, and his father was a leading scenic artist. 'A.C.', as he was commonly known, joined Poole's Theatres Ltd in 1882, as a scenic artist. During his long time with the company, he had many and various roles, including artist, engineer, architect, producer, and theatre and cinema manager. Many of the best myrioramas (panoramic scenes painted on large canvases which were scrolled past the viewer) were designed and painted by him. Some of his works proved strangely prophetic, such as *Contest in the Clouds*, which had scenes depicting aircraft guns, searchlights and airships.

Rogers was the first manager for Poole's of the old Albert Theatre, afterwards known as King's, which opened in Gloucester in 1891. Subsequently, he ran Poole's Studios in Worcester Street. In 1909 he moved to Ipswich, to open the first cinema there, but was back in Gloucester from 1914 to 1929. He then worked in Edinburgh before going back to Ipswich, and finally retired in 1940, having spent fifty-eight years with the same employers. At the time of his death, his eldest son was carrying on the family's theatrical tradition, being the general manager of the Gloucester Hippodrome. (*Gloucester Journal*)

MARCH 12TH

1860: A new museum was opened in Southgate Street by the Mayor, accompanied by members of the Corporation and of the Literary and Scientific Association. The party proceeded from the Tolsey to the museum building, where the Mayor addressed those assembled. He said that the opportunity of forming a public museum had arisen from the kindness of Mr Dobell (the poet, Sydney Dobell), who had given the use of the building for three years, free of charge.

Various gentlemen had donated objects of interest. Mr John Jones in particular, as well as giving his time and interest to the project, had donated geological specimens, a collection of land and water shells chiefly from the Gloucester area, and a series of drawings illustrating the history of the Egyptian mummy. Captain Guise had given a collection of shells, and Mr Barwick Baker had donated a beautiful collection of stuffed birds. Mr Wintle had given books on natural history, while the Revd Lysons had contributed a leaden coffin recently found near the city. Mr Bathurst had given geological models. The museum was to be open three days a week, on Tuesday, Thursday and Saturday, from 12 till 4 during the day, and from 6 till 8 in the evening. (*The Era*)

MARCH 13TH

1947: Following days of heavy snow, a great and rapid thaw, which began the night before, caused flooding in the city of Gloucester. A raging torrent flowed over the roads, and the Spa Ground was completely under water. Millions of gallons of water had flooded houses and made roads almost impassable. Thousands of acres of land surrounding the city were covered in water.

It was feared that the rapidly rising Severn would soon cause further flooding, and by the following night its waters were going over the Quay wall. Conditions were not helped when Gloucester was battered by gales on the night of March 16th. The waters continued to rise, and on March 20th families had to be evacuated, although some refused to leave their homes. By the next day, an official estimate was given that 500 homes were flooded. After a week, the waters were receding, and on March 29th it was reported that there had been the biggest drop in flood levels since the receding began. (*The Citizen*)

MARCH 14TH

1885: At the County Petty Sessions, held in Gloucester, George Pocket was summonsed for attempting to kill a salmon with an improper instrument, at Hempstead. William Watkins, a water bailiff, stated that on the day in question he had seen a salmon floating down the river tail first. He saw the defendant fire at it with a gun and the fish then disappeared. A witness said he saw the salmon, which rose to the surface at intervals, and he heard the report of a gun, but did not see who fired it. The defendant admitted firing the gun, but said he did not know he was shooting at a salmon; he thought it was some kind of water bird. The Bench dismissed the case. (*The Citizen*)

MARCH 15TH

1644: The House of Lords ratified an ordinance passed by the House of Commons on February 21st, which stated that 'one third part of the profit that shall arise out of the Customes payable upon currans shall be appropriated to the Garrison of Gloucester'. Orders made in 1642 which prohibited the importation of currants had been repealed, so that this fund-raising scheme could go ahead. (*Acts and Orders of the Interregnum*, ed. C.H. Firth and R.S. Rait, 1911)

———— • ◆ • ————

1904: A libel action brought by Dr Hadwen of Gloucester against Mr Price, a surgeon until recently practicing in Gloucester, was tried at Birmingham Assizes. Hadwen, who was a prominent campaigner against vaccinating for smallpox, had carried out a post-mortem on a child he had treated for a chill, and certified the cause of death as congestion of the brain and convulsions. The child's mother then developed symptoms of smallpox. Mr Price had written to the Chairman of the Sanitary Committee, complaining that the only other person at the post-mortem had been Hadwen's son, a medical student. The judge decided that Dr Hadwen should have called in an independent doctor for the post-mortem, but Mr Price's letter had contained some inaccuracies. The jury returned a verdict in favour of Dr Hadwen, and awarded him damages of one farthing. (*The Citizen*)

MARCH 16TH

1948: About 200 children attended a 'Safety First' fancy dress ball at the Guildhall, held for members of the *Gloucester Journal*'s Safety First Club. The Assembly Room had been decorated for the occasion, with road safety signs on the walls and two illuminated Belisha Beacons on the stage, and two almost full size 'Stop' and 'Go' traffic lights on each side of the staircase leading to the stage. The main table in the tea room was dominated by a huge iced cake, decorated with a street scene, including model traffic, trees, road signs and a telephone kiosk.

The children were greeted on their arrival by the City Sheriff and his wife, and by Mr Oakey, Chairman of the Gloucester Accident Prevention Council. Later in the evening, the Sheriff told the children that the road safety campaign was already beginning to show good results, but they were relying on them all to help in the task by sticking to the rules of the road at all times.

First prize for the boys in the fancy dress competition was awarded to David Finch, as a policeman, and second prize went to Donald Essex, whose costume represented the Highway Code. For the girls, first prize went to Joan Martin, who was a Belisha Crossing, and second prize went to Jill Smith, who was 'The Angel Who Forgot to Look Both Ways'. (*Gloucester Journal*)

MARCH 17TH

1986: The New Olympus Theatre was opened as the new base of the Gloucester Operatic and Dramatic Society (GODS), housed in a former bingo club, in Barton Street. The building had an interesting history, starting out in 1923 as the Picturedrome cinema. In 1933, it was acquired by Associated British Cinemas. ABC installed cinemascope, modernised the building and renamed it The Ritz in 1955. The cinema closed in April 1961, but when another picture house closed soon afterwards, the owners were asked to reconsider, and the Ritz was re-opened by the Mayor in June 1961. Its days as a cinema were numbered, however, and in 1962 it became a bingo club. In 1984, the bingo club closed. The GODS later bought the building and refurbished it.

As well as being the home of the GODS, the New Olympus served as a venue for the local community. In the year 2000, it started showing films again. (Moore, A., *The Picture Palaces of Gloucester and Cheltenham*, 1989)

MARCH 18TH

1963: The Beatles played at the Gloucester Regal Cinema, when they were on the verge of becoming superstars. They were on a UK tour with other artists, and had started off at the bottom of the bill, but by the time of the Gloucester show, they had been promoted to third from the top, behind Tommy Roe and the headline act, Chris Montez. Below the Beatles in the line-up were the Viscounts, the Terry Young Six, and Debbie Lee, and the compere was Tony Marsh. The group played songs including *I Saw Her Standing There*, *Love Me Do*, *Do You Want To Know A Secret?*, and *Please Please Me*.

The Citizen reporter, Hugh Worsnip, gave the band a favourable write-up, but this part of his report was cut from the final copy. A female member of the audience gained most of the headlines after she toppled into the orchestra pit while trying to throw chocolates to Chris Montez. (www.bradfordtimeline. co.uk; *The Citizen*)

MARCH 19TH

1878: Gloucester Vegetarian Society, inaugurated in this year, held a meeting at the Dock Coffee Rooms. Persons who were 'interested in the question' were invited to attend. The Vegetarian Society had started up nationally in 1847, but it took thirty-one years for a Gloucester branch to be formed. (*The Citizen*; www.veg.soc.org)

———— ◆ • ————

1941: In the early hours of the morning, an enemy aircraft circled round the Gloucester area for over an hour. The city had already suffered its first bomb attacks in January of this year, and it was feared that another raid was coming, but this plane seemed to be looking for something. It was thought most likely that it was trying to locate the exact position of the Gloster Aircraft Company. (Rennison, J., *Wings over Gloucestershire*, 1988)

MARCH 20TH

1937: Two submarines arrived in Gloucester Docks, having come up through the Gloucester & Berkeley Canal. They had arrived at Sharpness that afternoon and left for the 17-mile trip up the canal at 2 o'clock, finally reaching their destination as dusk was falling. They had been scheduled to arrive two days before, but bad weather on the south coast, from where they set off, had delayed them. The submarines were the H33, commanded by Lieutenant St Clair Ford, and the H49, commanded by Lieutenant H.J. Forbes. Second in command of the H33 was Lieutenant A.F. Collett, whose father, Colonel J.H. Collett, a member of the Gloucester Development Committee, had been instrumental in arranging the visit.

The submarines arrived on a Saturday, and members of the public were allowed to go on board from Sunday. The crowds on that day were so great that there were fears that people would be pushed into the water. The visitors left on the following Thursday. Photographs in the *Gloucester Journal* showed the commanders with the Mayor and Mayoress, the submarines going past Frampton-on-Severn, and members of the crew at a smoking concert (a concert where smoking was permitted) at the Guildhall. (*Gloucester Journal*)

March 21st

1906: An annual boxing competition was held by Gloucester Gymnastic and Boxing Club, at the Public Baths. Preliminary heats had already taken place between contestants from various local clubs, and this event was to decide the final winners. Mr I. Englishmann acted as referee. The contests were between pairs matched up according to weight, the lightest man weighing 7 stone 6lbs, and the heaviest weighing 11 stone. Two exhibitions were also shown, the first being 'The Englishmann Midgets' – the sons of the referee, Mike, aged 9, and Jack, aged 7, who put on a lively show, although their heads did not come up to the top of the ropes. The second was by rugby footballer Gordon Vears and Harry Mansfield, a professional boxer, who put on 'a splendid show'. A novelty was introduced in the form of a wrestling match between M.M. Henri Wansart and Henri L. Frope, two French members of the gymnasium, who fought in the Graeco-Roman style. After a fine struggle lasting 4 minutes 30 seconds, Wansart was awarded the win. The final event was a six-round wind-up between Jack Ward of Gloucester and Dick Holland of Birmingham, who both weighed 9 stone 2lbs. Ward knocked Holland out in the first round, after 35 seconds (*The Citizen*)

MARCH 22ND

1860: The Roman Catholic church in Northgate Street was publicly opened by the Hon. Revd W. Clifford, Bishop of Clifton. Although building work was not complete, enough had been finished to allow divine service to be held there. The building, in the Gothic style of the Second Period, had been designed by Gilbert Blount, a London architect, and the builders were Messrs Wingate of Clarence Street. The chancel, Lady Chapel, sacristy and about two thirds of the nave and aisles had been finished. A tower and a porch were still to be added.

Admission to the opening service was by ticket, and by 11 o'clock in the morning the church was filled by a respectable congregation, many of them influential Catholics who had travelled considerable distances to attend. There were also some Protestants present. The procession was composed of Dr Clifford, several members of the Chapter of Clifton, the Prior of Belmont Monastery, the Sub Prior and several Dominican monks of Woodchester, and a number of priests from the surrounding district. St Peter's was built on the site of an existing church. Building work began in 1859, and the completed church was consecrated in 1868. (*Cheltenham Chronicle*)

March 23rd

1894: This was Good Friday, and the weather was beautiful. Lots of visitors had come to Gloucester, many by train, from Birmingham, Bristol and South Wales. The main attraction was the Severn Bore, which was expected to be one of the highest of the season.

One of the visitors was Mr W. Glass from Bristol. He had come to Gloucester with two friends, and they decided to charter a small boat and row down the river to meet the bore. They hired a boat from Mr Priday at Westgate Bridge and engaged a man to row them. When they reached the Hempsted fish house, they met the full force of the high tide and the boat got into difficulties, throwing its occupants into the water. The boatman managed to swim ashore and two of the visitors were rescued by another boat, but Glass disappeared under the water and did not resurface. In the afternoon, several attempts were made to drag for the body, without success. It was thought likely that it had been taken down the river. (*The Citizen*)

MARCH 24TH

1786: Richard Meek of Barton Street, a gardener, appeared before magistrates for failing to clean his ditches, adjoining the turnpike road, near Barton Street. The complainant was Nathaniel King, the turnpike surveyor. Meek was unwell, so his wife appeared in his place. He was fined 10 shillings. (*Calendar of Summary Convictions at Petty Sessions, 1781-1837*, ed. I. Wyatt, Gloucestershire Record Series, Volume 22, 2008)

———◆———

1939: The town council made an application to the city magistrates, for authority to close two small alleys, known as Soot Alley and St Aldate Square, as part of a scheme to improve King's Square. The Town Clerk said a new 40-foot road was to be constructed, and that all old property lying on the north side of the square would be demolished, leaving St Aldate Street open to King's Square. The city's largest store, Bonmarché, was to be considerably extended, and a new cinema built on the site of the old St John's burial ground in St Aldate Street. The magistrates granted the order. (*Cheltenham Chronicle*)

———◆———

1907: At the Glevum Hall, Mrs Despard, a prominent suffragette, gave a lecture on 'Shelley, the poet of the Revolution'. (*The Citizen*)

MARCH 25TH

1897: To commemorate the Diamond Jubilee of Queen Victoria, the Mayor of Gloucester planted an English oak tree in the public park. He expressed the hope that the 'Jubilee Tree' would grow upward and branch outwards, symbolic of the prosperity and success of the nation. After the ceremony, the party proceeded to the Guildhall for lunch, followed by more festivities. (*The Citizen*)

———◆———

1935: The Plaza Cinema opened in Eastgate Street. In 1957, it became the Odeon, and, along with the Regal in King's Square, gained a reputation for staging live acts. It was the last cinema in Gloucester to have a Wurlitzer organ. In 1975, it was converted into a bingo hall, which it remains at the time of writing. (www. cinematopia.co.uk)

MARCH 26TH

1867: An indenture was drawn up between Samuel J. Moreland, a Gloucester timber merchant, and Henry Jacobs, establishing a match-making factory in Gloucester, at premises adjoining the Gloucester & Berkeley Canal on Bristol Road. Moreland had formerly supplied Bryant and May with waste wood to make matches, until he had a disagreement with the company and decided to start making matches himself. He moved his business to a new site on Bristol Road in 1868, and stayed there for over a hundred years. In 1913, Moreland's, by then the manufacturers of the famous 'England's Glory' brand, was taken over by Bryant and May, although the family continued to manage the business. The factory finally closed in 1976. (Campion, P., *England's Glory: The Moreland Story*, 2005)

1994: A celebration of 300 years of service by the Gloucestershire Regiment was held in Gloucester. The event started with a service of thanksgiving at the Cathedral, followed by a parade at the Docks, at which the regiment's colours were marched off parade for the last time. After the parade, a lunch was held at Innsworth. On April 27th, the regiment was amalgamated into the Royal Gloucestershire, Berkshire and Wiltshire Regiment. (www.glosters.org.uk)

MARCH 27TH

1884: Samuel Bowley, a prominent Gloucester Quaker, was buried. Born in Cirencester in 1802 and educated at the Quaker school in Nailsworth, Bowley moved to Gloucester after he married and became a cheese factor. He was to become a prominent member of Gloucester society, being chairman of many local organisations. He was perhaps best known as an advocate of temperance, believing it was important to educate the masses about the evils of drink. He was one of the early founders of the Friends' Temperance Union, and became president of the National Temperance League. He died on March 23rd 1884, on his 82nd birthday. His funeral was attended by the Mayor and Corporation, and hundreds of people lined the streets to see the hearse, followed by carriages of mourners, make its way to the cemetery. (*Oxford Dictionary of National Biography*; *The Citizen*)

———◆———

1934: Sir Oswald Moseley came to Gloucester to address a meeting, organised by the Gloucester branch of the British Union of Fascists. Followers of Moseley, of both sexes, lined the entrance to Shire Hall, and were prominent in the Assembly Hall, giving the speaker the fascist salute as he mounted the platform. However, it was obvious that many in the audience were not supporters of the cause, although they listened to Moseley politely. On the following day, Moseley appeared in Cheltenham. (*Cheltenham Chronicle*)

MARCH 28TH

1741: Thomas Raikes, son of Robert Raikes senior, the founder of the *Gloucester Journal*, was born in Gloucester. While his brother, Robert junior, made his name in Gloucester, Thomas went to London, where, eventually, he was to become Governor of the Bank of England, holding the position from 1797 to 1799. He was a friend of Prime Minister William Pitt the Younger, and of William Wilberforce. He died in Middlesex in 1813. (*Oxford Dictionary of National Biography*)

1902: The annual dinner of the Gloucester Branch of the Associated Society of Locomotive Engineers and Firemen took place at the Windmill Hotel. After dinner, a toast list, interspersed with songs, was gone through.

The Chairman proposed a toast to 'The Associated Society of Engineers and Firemen', and spoke of the advantages and value of such an organisation, advising those present who were not already members to join. He congratulated the branch on gaining seven new members, and said the Society as a whole, in the last year, had acquired 931 new members, making a total membership of 10,050. Mr W. Green said the sick fund had been drawn on frequently last year, which encroached heavily on the branch's funds. (*The Citizen*)

MARCH 29TH

1881: After an investigation into the election of 1880, in which Thomas Robinson was elected and then removed as Member of Parliament for Gloucester City, the report of the Election Commission into Corruption and Bribery was published on this day. The commission into bribery in Gloucester had begun in October 1880 and sat for many weeks, listening to evidence from those who had played an active part in the election campaign.

The commissioners now reported that the leading agents engaged in corrupt practices on both sides were principally members of the Corporation. The practice of bribery was so ingrained in the city that many of the poorer electors did not use their vote unless they were paid. It was calculated that, during this election, nearly 300 people had distributed bribes among 2,756 electors. The bribers included six magistrates, one member of the School Board, several Guardians of the Poor, and town councillors. The conclusion of the report was that bribery was the rule and not the exception at all elections in the city. No great blame appears to have been attached to Thomas Robinson himself, probably because the report revealed what was already widely known – that everyone involved in the election had been guilty of corruption. Robinson was elected as the city's MP again in 1887, and was knighted in June 1894. (*The Citizen*; *The Graphic*)

MARCH 30TH

1750: John Stafford Smith, son of Martin and Agrilla Smith, was baptised at Gloucester Cathedral, where his father was organist. He was educated at the Cathedral School, then became a choirboy at the Chapel Royal, London. Inheriting his father's musical gift, he played as organist at the Three Choirs Festival in 1790. A fine organist and composer, he is best known for composing the tune which became the National Anthem of the United States of America. The words of *The Star Spangled Banner* were written in 1812 by Francis Scott Key. Smith originally composed the tune in 1780, as the constitutional song of the Anachreonic Society, called *To Anchreon in Heaven*. (Gloucestershire Archives, transcript of Cathedral Baptisms; www.visit-gloucestershire.co.uk)

MARCH 31ST

1742: At about 10 o'clock in the morning, James Matthews was executed outside the City Gaol, for horse-stealing. Although many hangings had taken place at the county's execution site at Over, outside the city, this was the first hanging within the city's walls for thirty-seven years. It was reported that after he was condemned to death at the assizes, Matthews twice tried to escape from the gaol. He had previously escaped from two other prisons and was described in the press as a 'notorious offender'. He refused to confess to the crime for which he died, until the moment he was 'turned off'. (*Gloucester Journal*)

April 1st

1301: A fire broke out at the church of Llanthony Priory. The building was gutted, leaving only the walls standing. (Langston, J.N., 'Priors of Llanthony by Gloucester', in *Transactions of the Bristol and Gloucestershire Archaeological Society*, Volume 63).

———◆·———

1554: James Brooks was consecrated as Bishop of Gloucester, by the Bishops of Winchester, London and Durham. He was to be the last Catholic Bishop of the diocese. Brooks was born in Hampshire in 1512. He was chosen by Queen Mary to replace the unfortunate Bishop Hooper in the see of Gloucester. In 1558, Mary died and was succeeded on the throne by her half-sister, Elizabeth, a Protestant. Brooks refused to sign the Oath of Supremacy, and was deprived of his office and sent to gaol. He died, still in prison, in 1560, and was buried in Gloucester Cathedral, without a monument. (*Oxford Dictionary of National Biography*)

April 2nd

1787: Workmen began to pull down the walls of the old castle, to make way for the construction of a new County Prison. The prisoners were put into temporary accommodation while the new prison was being built. The need for a new prison had been made evident by the reports of the prison reformer John Howard, who visited Gloucester three times between 1777 and 1784. Howard had criticised the overcrowded and insanitary conditions in the castle. The new prison was to put inmates into separate cells and divide them into different classes, which were not permitted to interact. The prisoners moved into the new buildings in July 1791. (*Gloucester Journal*; Whiting, J.R.S., *Prison Reform in Gloucestershire, 1776-1820,* 1975)

———◆———

1889: An inquest was held at the Infirmary on William Beard, aged 77, who had died after being hit by a horse-drawn vehicle while crossing Northgate Street. It appeared that Beard had stepped out from the front of a tram and into the path of a trap, being driven by Mrs Wasley. He was hit by the wheel shaft of the trap and knocked down. He was taken to the Infirmary, where he died, having suffered broken ribs and an injury to a lung. A verdict of accidental death was returned, and no blame was attached to Mrs Wasley. (*The Citizen*)

April 3rd

1820: Due to the extreme severity of the weather, not a single head of cattle was put up for sale at Gloucester cattle market on this day. (*Morning Post*)

———— ◆ ————

1867: Charles Dickens gave one of his famous readings at the Theatre Royal, Gloucester. Despite the price of tickets being doubled, the occasion attracted a large and fashionable audience to the theatre. Dickens chose for his readings *Doctor Marigold*, the story of a remarkable Cheap Jack, and the Trial Scene from *Pickwick Papers*. A press reporter was of the opinion that Dickens was 'somewhat lacking in power as a reader', but said that his rendering of the first reading was a wonderful piece of acting. 'The Trial of Mr Pickwick' was equally successful, and was very appropriate on this occasion, as the assizes were being held in Gloucester and some of the audience were barristers, and, it was rumoured, one of the judges was also present. (*Gloucester Journal*)

APRIL 4TH

1942: Two German bombers attacked the Gloster Aircraft Company's works, hitting the factory and the surrounding area of Brockworth and Hucclecote. It was Easter weekend, and the dayshift was just leaving the factory – at about half past four in the afternoon – when the raid began. Lots of people were out in the open as six bombs were dropped. One scored a direct hit on a bus in the car park. The damage was terrible, with glass and splinters flying over a wide area. Two more attacks were to follow. A house near the factory was hit and all five occupants, including a 10-month-old baby, were killed. In the factory itself, a canteen and a shop were wrecked, and fire in the buildings took several hours to extinguish. In total, ten men, five women and three children were killed, and between 100 and 200 people were injured. (Rennison, J., *Wings Over Gloucestershire*, 1988)

❖

1865: A notice of bankruptcy was published on Samuel Henry Hayward of the city of Gloucester, Pharmaceutical Chemist, Sauce Manufacturer and Pickle Merchant, trading in partnership with George Stewart, under the name of S.H. Hayward & Co. Ltd. (*London Gazette*)

APRIL 5TH

1894: A memorial stone was laid at the site of the Linden Road Board School, where building work had begun in September 1893. The school, which would hold 813 pupils, was being built to meet the needs of the rapidly increasing population in the south of the city. It was to be a mixed school, but with separate entrances for boys and girls on either side of the headmaster's office, and separate playgrounds. The infants would have their own department, but would share the girls' playground. Over the girls' cloakroom there would be a cooking department, which girls from other schools would be able to access. Over the boys' cloakroom would be the caretaker's quarters. There was to be a central hall, with classrooms surrounding it, and private rooms for the teachers, with windows overlooking the two playgrounds.

Under the memorial stone, a glass bottle was placed, containing copies of *The Times*, *Gloucester Journal*, *The Citizen* and the *Gloucestershire Chronicle*, a copy of the inscription on the memorial stone, and various coins of the realm. The school opened in September 1895. (*The Citizen*)

APRIL 6TH

1900: A shocking accident took place at the Midland Railway Station. William Joseph Butler, a carriage cleaner, aged 17, attempted to board a passenger train which was engaged in shunting operations, but missed his footing and fell between the platform and the train. One of his arms was crushed, and the wheels of the carriage passed over his right leg. He was taken to the Infirmary, where both his injured limbs had to be amputated.

Another accident took place at Fielding and Platt's on the same afternoon. John Adams, a moulder's labourer, was in the yard where moulding boxes were stacked, when one of them, made of a huge mass of metal with iron plates, fell on him. It took fifty of his workmates to extract him, with the help of a pulley-jack, which hoisted the metal off him. He was taken to the Infirmary, where it was found that both his legs were broken. (*The Citizen*)

1787: This was Good Friday, and at the request of the Bishop, the Mayor had sent officers to notify the city that Good Friday was to be set apart for religious worship, and no shops should open. Most of the businesses complied. (*Gloucester Journal*)

APRIL 7TH

1933: The annual spring sale of pedigree and cross-breed pigs was held at Gloucester market, and attracted a larger number of entries than at any previous sale. Opening the proceedings, Mr G. Norman Bruton said that everything was being done to encourage the breeding of the right kind of pigs, and it was a significant fact that Gloucester market had an annual turnover of over 100,000 pigs. Top price in the sale was realised by a large white boar, the property of Mr Young of King's Norton, which made £14 10s 6d. (*The Citizen*)

———◆———

1882: Opening services were held at the newly-built Barton Street Primitive Methodist Raikes' Memorial Chapel and Schools. Morning and afternoon services took place, and a public tea was provided in the evening, with 600 people fed over three sittings in the schoolroom. At 7 o'clock, a public meeting was held in the chapel, which was filled to capacity, and extra benches had to be provided. The Mayor, Alderman A.G. Jones, presided. The meeting started with singing, readings and prayers, then the Mayor congratulated the congregation on the character of the building they had erected. Reverend J. Dinnick, pastor of the chapel, recalled the time when the Primitive Methodists started, twenty-seven years previously, with ten members. There were now over 7,000 churches connected to the body. (*The Citizen*)

APRIL 8TH

1941: The first British and Allied Jet aeroplane did a taxi run and made a few short hops at Hucclecote. George Carter of the Gloster Aircraft Company had built the Gloster E28/39 using the jet engine designed by Frank Whittle, at the request of the War Ministry. The aeroplane flew properly for the first time at RAF Cranwell on May 15th. The War Ministry then asked for the E29/39 to be converted into a fighter plane. Carter realised that it would only be able to operate as a fighter if it had two engines, and adapted the design accordingly. The plane began ground trials in July 1942. The F9/40, as it was numbered, was to become the *Meteor*. (James, D.N., *Gloster Aircraft Company*, 1994)

❖

1805: A notice addressed to the Ladies of Gloucester appeared in the *Gloucester Journal*, drawing their attention to Dixon's Anti-Billious Pills. They were for the treatment of billious and gouty disorders, nervous and sick headaches, heartburn, etc. The pills, which were patronised by the Royal Family and most of the Nobility, were now on sale from D. Walker, the printer of the newspaper, at his new medicine warehouse in Westgate Street, and from C. Jones in Southgate Street. (*Gloucester Journal*)

APRIL 9TH

1867: For many months, Gloucester had been raising funds to purchase a lifeboat, which would be stationed at some dangerous part of the coast; £500 had been raised and a boat had been purchased. On this day, the lifeboat was launched at the Docks. At two o'clock a very long procession formed, which included the Mayor and Corporation. The lifeboat was drawn along on its carriage by a team of horses.

At the Docks, the Dean, the Mayor and Mayoress and the Corporation stood on a platform as the boat was put in position. The chairman of the Lifeboat Committee asked Captain Ward, as representative of the Lifeboat Institution, to accept the boat as a gift from the city. It had been decided that the boat should be stationed at Falmouth. The Dean said a prayer and the Chaplain of the Mariner's Chapel recited the Lord's Prayer, then the Mayoress, Mrs Robinson, stepped forward to break a bottle of wine on the stern, saying, 'I name this boat the *Gloucester*. God prosper her!' In a few minutes, the boat was got ready and was shot over the basin wall into the water. It was then rolled over and righted itself. The lifeboat arrived at Falmouth on April 13th. (*Western Daily Press*)

April 10th

1887: A bitter wind blew through Gloucester on this Easter Sunday morning, but this didn't stop people from attending the services at the various churches and chapels. The artillery, headed by the band, marched to the Cathedral, where a large congregation listened to an impressive service. Joyful music rang through the building and the choir, according to *The Citizen*, 'sang better than usual'.

The altar was decorated with vases of choice flowers, and a processional hymn was sung. The Dean preached in the morning, and the Bishop took the service in the evening, which was equally well attended. There was also a special Nave service, at which the Dean again preached. At this latter service, selections from the *Messiah* were performed, and the choristers were worked extremely hard. (*The Citizen*)

APRIL 11TH

1592: A case was heard in a Court of Audience before the Archbishop of Canterbury, to resolve a dispute between the Bishop of Gloucester, John Bullingham, and his Chancellor of the Consistory Court, William Blackleech (or Blackleach). Since 1589, the Bishop had been trying to get rid of Blackleech, who had gained a reputation for being a corrupt judge in the consistory court, but the Chancellor refused to be ousted. The row led to the pair holding separate church courts, with the one presided over by Blackleech being the more popular, as he was known to let miscreants off with a fine (which was rumoured to go into his own pocket), rather than making them do public penance.

The hearing on April 11th 1592 resulted in a compromise settlement, and Blackleech was still Chancellor when Bullingham died in May 1598. The next Bishop, Godfrey Goldsborough, also argued with the Chancellor, who last sat as a judge in April 1600, but continued to issue marriage licences. Blackleech died in 1616 and was buried in the Cathedral. (Price, F.D., 'Bishop Bullingham and Chancellor Blackleech: A Diocese Divided', in *Transactions of the Bristol and Gloucestershire Archaeological Society*, Volume 91)

APRIL 12TH

1896: The new Midland Railway Company station was opened in Gloucester. It was a handsome structure, of red brick with terracotta decoration, and cast-iron and glass awnings in a ridge-and-furrow design. It had three through platforms, and was connected by a long footbridge to the Great Western Railway station. Trains from the south came in to the new station via Tuffley junction and the 'Tuffley Loop'. This part of the line had four gated road crossings, including the Barton Gates crossing.

In the 1950s, the station was renamed 'Gloucester Eastgate'. It was finally closed down in December 1975, along with the Tuffley Loop. This meant that services which had previously stopped at Eastgate now had to reverse into the Central Station, an inconvenience which resulted in fewer trains stopping at Gloucester. (www.disused-stations.co.uk; *The Citizen*)

APRIL 13TH

1950: Seven men were injured in an explosion at the Gloster Aircraft Company factory in Brockworth. The *Meteor* jet fighter and trainer were being made here, and it was while one of the aircraft fuel tanks was being tested in the tinsmiths' department that it suddenly exploded and burst into flames. Five of the men who were most seriously hurt were taken to the City General Hospital, and two were kept in. James Herbert, of Moreton Valence, was described by the hospital as being dangerously ill, with burns and fractured arms. Joseph Bullock, of Prestbury, was also seriously ill, with burns. One worker who had a minor injury was treated and discharged at the Royal Infirmary. The seventh man was treated without going to hospital. (*Western Daily Press*)

1932: Mrs Stanley Baldwin, wife of the former Prime Minister, opened an Empire Fair in Shire Hall, organised by the Conservative Association. She said that she knew Gloucester well, because she used to accompany her husband when he attended board meetings as a director of the Gloucester Railway and Carriage Company. While he was busy, she used to wander round the city, and in particular liked to visit the Cathedral. (*Cheltenham Chronicle*)

APRIL 14TH

1890: At the City Petty Sessions, Joseph Hibbard was summonsed under the bye-laws of the Tramway Company for wilfully obstructing a tramcar. John Ireland, the driver, said he was going down Southgate Street when he came up to the defendant, driving a herd of cows. He asked him to move aside, but he refused and 'used bad language'. The tram was delayed by about eight minutes because of this. Ellen Wright, a passenger, said Hibbard was in a terrible passion and struck the tram-horse two or three times with a stick.

For the defence, Mr Merrett, the owner of the cattle, said they had come from Bristol and were very footsore, so he had cautioned the defendant to drive them carefully. He overtook the cattle by the Robinhood Inn, and with the help of another drover, cleared them off so the tram could go on. Hibbard was fined five shillings and costs. (*The Citizen*)

APRIL 15TH

1832: Herbert Vaughan, of an ancient and powerful Roman Catholic family based at Courtfield, Herefordshire, was born in Gloucester. He was the eldest son of Colonel John Vaughan and Eliza Rolls, who converted to Catholicism shortly before her marriage. The Vaughan's had thirteen children. All five of their daughters went into convents, while five of their eight sons became priests, and three of those rose to become Bishops. Herbert became the Right Reverend Herbert Vaughan, Roman Catholic Bishop of Salford. In 1892, he became the Archbishop of Westminster, and in 1893 he became a Cardinal. (*The Catholic Encyclopedia*)

———— • • ————

1878: At Gloucester Assizes, William Williams, a 36-year-old boatman, was charged with bigamy. He was married at Gloucester in 1869 but later deserted his wife and their three children. In November 1877, he returned to Gloucester and became acquainted with a widow named Wells, who had four children. He moved in with her and they were later married. The jury found him guilty, but recommend him to be treated leniently, 'because of the behaviour of the second wife'. He was sentenced to one month in prison. (*Western Mail*)

April 16th

1902: Gloucester Cricket Club held its Annual General Meeting. Mr A.W. Vears presided at the New Inn Hotel, where there was a fair attendance of members. In opening the meeting, the chairman spoke of the death of a mainstay of the club, Mr Boughton. A resolution was drawn up to express the loss they all felt at the death of their late captain, and to convey to Mrs Boughton and family their heartfelt sympathy. A donation of five guineas from club funds was voted to go to the Boughton Memorial Fund.

The Balance Sheet was then examined and adopted, and the officers and the captains of the First XI, Second XI, and the Thursday Second XI were elected. The Mayor of Gloucester, Councillor S. Bland, was unanimously re-elected President. Mr Canning Robins was re-elected as Honorary Secretary. He appealed for the hearty and loyal support of every member of the club in the coming season. (*The Citizen*)

———— • ◆ • ————

1787: It was reported in the *Gloucester Journal* that the County Prison had been greatly relieved by the transportation over the last few days of thirty to forty criminals, who were bound for Botany Bay. Until the ships were ready to sail, the prisoners were to be kept on the hulks at Portsmouth and Plymouth. (*Gloucester Journal*)

APRIL 17TH

2003: This was Maundy Thursday, and Gloucester had a visit from Queen Elizabeth II. The Queen, who was then 77 years old, came to the Cathedral to distribute specially minted Maundy Money to seventy-seven men and seventy-seven women. Those receiving the money were pensioners, chosen for their services to the Church and the community. The oldest recipient was 99-year-old Doris Judd. This was the first time that the Maundy Money ceremony had taken place at Gloucester Cathedral.

The Queen, accompanied by Prince Philip, walked from Shire Hall to the Cathedral, cheered by hundreds of onlookers. They stopped to chat to well-wishers, and the Queen was presented with posies by children. The spectators were also treated to the sight of The Yeomen of the Guard, the Queen's ceremonial bodyguard, in their scarlet and gold uniforms, marching down Westgate Street.

The tradition of the sovereign distributing Maundy Money dates back to at least the thirteenth century, in the reign of Edward I. Originally, in an act of humility, the monarch would wash the feet of the recipients, but James II (who reigned from 1685 to 1688) was the last to do this. The ceremony used to take place only in London, but Queen Elizabeth II decided it should be done in a different cathedral or abbey every year. (*The Citizen*; www.royal.gov.uk)

APRIL 18TH

1818: Six men were hanged in Gloucester on the same morning. Five of the prisoners were executed on the gatehouse roof at the County Prison; the other was hanged outside the City Prison in Southgate Street. All had been tried at the recent assizes. John Hayward, a butcher from Mitcheldean, was condemned for sheep-stealing; Joseph Ingram received the death sentence for assaulting a little girl near Bristol; Thomas Bishop and William Mason, from Fullbrook, near Burford in Oxfordshire, were found guilty of a variety of offences, the most serious being sheep-stealing; Henry Barnes had been tried at the County Assizes for stealing from a house in Hartpury, after escaping from the City Gaol.

The crime for which Joseph Richards was condemned at the City Assizes was an unusual one. He had tried to blackmail a surgeon at the Infirmary, threatening to accuse him of trying to commit 'an unnatural act' while fitting him with a truss, if he didn't give him money. While the five other men died together at the County Prison, Richards faced his end alone.

There might have been a seventh execution on this day, as Ann Tye had also been condemned to die at the County Assizes, for infanticide. However, her sentence was respited, and she was not hanged until May 4th. (Evans, J., *Hanged at Gloucester*, 2011)

APRIL 19TH

1876: Samuel Sebastian Wesley, organist at Gloucester Cathedral, died at his residence in Palace Yard. He was the grandson of the famous Methodist preacher and composer, Charles Wesley. Born in London in 1810, he was the son of Samuel Wesley, a talented musician and composer. S.S. Wesley inherited his family's musical gifts and became an organist, his first position being at St James's Chapel in Hampstead Road, London, when he was only 15 years old. In July 1832, he became organist at Hereford Cathedral. Three years later, having married the sister of the Dean of Hereford, he moved to Exeter to be organist there. He was also the organist at Leeds parish church and Winchester Cathedral, before he moved to Gloucester in 1865.

In Gloucester, he became well known as the Cathedral organist and the conductor at the Three Choirs Festival. He remained in the city for the rest of his life, but was not buried there, having asked that he be laid to rest in Exeter, next to his only daughter. (*Oxford Dictionary of National Biography*)

APRIL 20TH

1571: It was announced in Gloucester Cathedral that the Bishop, Richard Cheyney, had been excommunicated. Cheyney had been consecrated as Bishop of Gloucester in 1562. In the following year, he wrote to Cecil, Queen Elizabeth I's Secretary of State, complaining that puritanism was rampant in his diocese and stating that he would like to resign. He stayed at Gloucester, though, and became popular with the people for his liberality. Cheyney was excommunicated for refusing to subscribe to the Thirty-Nine Articles (which defined the doctrine of the Church of England). The Archdeacon of Gloucester, Guy Elton, was given the task of publishing the excommunication. The punishment did not last for too long though, as Cheyney was absolved on May 12th, and kept his position at Gloucester. He died on April 29th 1579, and was buried in the Cathedral. (*Oxford Dictionary of National Biography*)

APRIL 21ST

1892: *The Citizen* reported that the Dean of Gloucester, Dr Spencer, had printed, for private circulation, an account of an important discovery he believed he had made, namely that the remains of King Osric, the founder of Gloucester Abbey, were buried beneath his shrine in the Cathedral. Because Osric, King of Northumbria, died in the year 729 and the shrine was not built until the sixteenth century, it had always been assumed that Osric was buried elsewhere in the Abbey. The Dean, however, had read Leland's account of his visit to the Abbey in 1540, when he wrote that Osric's remains had been moved from the Lady Chapel and placed under a tomb bearing his name, on the north side of the High Altar. The shrine to Osric, built by the last Abbot before the Abbey became a Cathedral in 1541, stood on the right-hand side of the High Altar, in the Choir.

Two side panels were removed from the memorial and a leaden coffin was found, containing some very ancient remains, which were left untouched. The Dean believed that the lead coffin was probably a replacement of a more ancient stone loculus, and the discovery meant that Gloucester held the oldest known remains of a Saxon king. (*The Citizen*)

APRIL 22ND

1961: The Gaumont Cinema closed on this day, after an eventful history as a picture house. Originally called the City Cinema, it had opened in 1911 in Eastgate Street, on the site of the Rising Sun public house. Improvements were made to the premises a few years later, and it re-opened in March 1915 as The Hippodrome. In 1922, it was acquired by the Poole family, who kept the venue open for over thirty years. In October 1955, the building was badly damaged by a fire, but the cinema was re-opened in June 1956, having being taken over by Rank, and was renamed The Gaumont. Nearly five years later, the old cinema closed down permanently. (Moore, A., *The Picture Palaces of Gloucester and Cheltenham*, 1989)

APRIL 23RD

1787: An advertisement appeared in the *Gloucester Journal* for 'The Cheap Gloucester Hat Warehouse'. John Daniels of Bristol had just opened a warehouse, nearly opposite the Bank in Northgate Street, where he had laid out a new and fashionable assortment of hats of every kind and quality: ladies' Habit Hats of various colours; mens' and boys' fine and course hats; and every article in the business for sale on such terms, 'that he flatters himself will merit the attention of the public'. (*Gloucester Journal*)

———◆———

1902: St George's Day was celebrated by the Corporation in Gloucester with a banquet at the New Inn Hotel. The Chair was occupied by Councillor C. Holbrook, supported by various councillors and aldermen. Apologies were received from the Mayor and the City High Sheriff. Mr Conway Jones provided each guest with a white rose button hole. After dinner, a toast was made to the Royal Family and the National Anthem was sung, before other toasts were proposed. Various guests then entertained the company with songs. A special guest, Mr H.W. Phipps, past Supreme Grand President of the Order of the Sons of St George in the USA, kindly showed the other guests his magnificent collection of orders, emblems and insignia. (*The Citizen*)

APRIL 24TH

1882: A gathering took place in the Masonic Hall, to celebrate the birthday of a well-known city missionary, David Griffin. The hall was filled and the company consisted of those poorer members of society who had been helped by Mr Griffin in his visits over the last seventeen years, and regarded him as a friend. There were also present representatives of practically every religious organisation in the city.

After tea, Alderman Jesse Sessions presided as speeches were made, bearing testimony to the devotion of Mr Griffin to his work. Mrs Sessions, on behalf of the women, many of whom were present, spoke of the kindness and help he had offered in times of sickness and sorrow, and wished him many happy returns of the day. Mr Griffin received a small remuneration for his work, made up from voluntary contributions, and it was now resolved to make him a present, towards which a large number of small sums from the many people who appreciated his labours had been received. (*The Citizen*)

APRIL 25TH

1892: Between 5 and 9 o'clock in the evening, the south end of Gloucester was the scene of a demonstration. The wife of a boatman had left her husband and seven children and eloped with another boatman. The happy couple had gone up the river in a longboat, and on their return, found a hostile reception waiting for them. A crowd had gathered on the quay, and effigies of the pair had been strung up on a crane and set alight. There were calls for the boatman to turn the woman out, but he denied that she was on board. Some people managed to get on board and found her curled up in the cabin. She was fetched onto the deck and doused in water.

The boatman managed to get to the other side of the basin and the pair got into a cab, which drove to Southgate Street. When they got there, they were met by a number of men and women who refused to let the cab go any further. A scuffle took place as the mob tried to get the couple out, and a window was broken. The cab driver then took his horse out of the shafts and left his passengers in the cab. Luckily, two policemen arrived soon afterwards, and the couple were rescued. (*The Citizen*)

April 26th

1827: The Gloucester & Sharpness Canal officially opened. A huge crowd gathered at the docks to watch the first two vessels enter the basin, amid the firing of guns and the ringing of church bells. Although Gloucester had been given the status of a port in 1580, it was difficult for vessels to navigate the shallow tidal stretch of the Severn when approaching the city. The opening of the canal allowed ships to bypass this stretch of river. As a result, considerable trade built up with foreign ports. (Conway-Jones, H., *Gloucester Docks: An Historical Guide*, 2009)

1836: James 'Jemmy' Wood, the Gloucester banker, was buried at St Mary de Crypt Church. Born in 1756, he had taken over the family business in 1802. He had gained a reputation as a miser, and became famous as a result of this. He died on April 20th 1836, leaving about £900,000 in his will, but disputes over it carried on for many years, until most of the money had gone on legal fees. On the day of his funeral, a large crowd gathered to watch the procession, but there was none of the respectful silence which was usually shown on these occasions. The *Gloucester Journal* reported that 'many of the crowd evinced a levity of demeanor quite inconsistent with the solemnity of the occasion'. (www.visit-gloucestershire.co.uk; *Gloucester Journal*)

APRIL 27TH

1904: On this day, a trial run of Gloucester's new electric tram system was made from the city centre to Hucclecote. The Mayor, the Chairman of the Tramways Committee, various councillors and civic officials and other dignitaries were on board. The route was thronged by crowds of spectators. The car stopped outside the Bell Hotel for photographs, then made for the Cross, where the points were successfully negotiated. There was a delay at the Worcester Street junction, because the points were open for the Kingsholm section, but the party soon continued on its way, passing under the London Road railway bridge without incident. Wotton Hill, always difficult for the horses on the old trams, was ascended without losing speed. The terminus at Hucclecote was reached in a little over half an hour from the start, and took only twenty minutes from the Worcester Street junction. On the return journey, the party stopped at Hucclecote House for champagne and cigars.

On May 4th, the tramline was officially opened, and on this occasion the leading car was driven by the Mayor, Alderman Blinkhorn. When the system was fully completed, the routes would be from Tuffley Avenue to Hucclecote, from Reservoir Road to the City Boundary, Wotton (via Stroud Road junction), Reservoir Road to Kingsholm (via Park End Road) and Cemetery Road to Westgate Bridge. (*The Citizen*)

APRIL 28TH

1948: At a meeting of Gloucester City Council, it was decided to name seven new roads First to Seventh Avenue, instead of using place names. Council member Mrs Wentworth said place names meant something to the citizens of Gloucester and the people who would occupy the houses. To her mind, the use of numbers, as recommended by the Highways Committee, savoured of looking to America. If she lived in Pitchcombe Avenue, for example, the name would conjure up the vision of the beautiful Cotswold village. She moved that the recommendation should be reconsidered. Mr N.S. Platt seconded.

Mr R.W. Smith declared that the suggestion of the Highways Committee was sound commonsense. Strangers and postal authorities would find the proposed system much more helpful. Mrs Wentworth had not explained what emotions would be roused by living in Quarry Road, he said, referring to one of the other place names suggested. Mr J.H. Edge said he could assure Mrs Wentworth that this was not a case of American encirclement. Mr R.E. Moulder believed that the majority of the people who lived in the roads would not be Gloucester people, and place names would have little significance for them. The amendment was defeated by nineteen votes to fourteen. (*Gloucester Journal*)

APRIL 29TH

1862: The first wedding for more than a century was celebrated at Gloucester Cathedral. The bride was Miss Mary Bankes, daughter of Revd Canon Bankes, and granddaughter of the Hon. Revd the Dean of Gloucester. The bridegroom was Mr Philip Pennant Pennant, of Bodfari, Flintshire. The ceremony was performed by the Bishop of Gloucester. At least 3,000 people were present, and the galleries were crowded. The assembly was thought to be larger than when the present Bishop preached his first sermon.

The 'young and lovely bride' was elegantly dressed, and attended by seven bridesmaids, who were her four sisters, the bridegroom's sister, and Miss Wiggin and Miss Fanny Bankes. After 'partaking of a handsome *dejeuner*', at which a large and fashionable party were assembled, the bride and groom left for Paris, to spend their honeymoon. (*Western Daily Press*)

APRIL 30TH

1890: The West of England Magpie Fanciers' Association held its monthly meeting at the Worcester Street Coffee Tavern. There was an excellent display of young birds, and Mr W. Sessions officiated as judge. Class 1 was for reds or yellows, bred 1890; Class 2 was for any colour and any age; and Class 3 was for blacks, bred 1890. Several birds received cards of commendation.

Letters were read from absent members, and the accounts were passed to be paid. Hearty votes of thanks were given to Mr Sessions for officiating as judge, and to Mr Moody for acting as chairman. (*The Citizen*)

MAY 1st

1876: The first edition of *The Citizen*, Gloucester's first daily newspaper, was published. It was an evening newspaper costing one halfpenny, and consisting of four pages of advertisements, national and international news and local intelligence. An editorial explained that it had become obvious that there was a need in Gloucester, with its importance as a city and port, for a more frequent supply of news than the weekly local newspapers could satisfy. *The Citizen* declared itself to be an advocate of Liberal principles. Although it recognised the excellent service provided by the existing weekly papers in Gloucester, an advertisement in this first issue announced that on the next Saturday the proprietors of *The Citizen* would publish a new weekly newspaper, to be called *The Gloucester Herald*, which would cost one penny.

The Citizen was founded by businessman Samuel Bland. In January 1879, Bland met with Thomas Chance, the owner of the *Gloucester Journal*, and they decided to combine their operations. The *Gloucester Journal* continued to be published as a weekly paper. In 1924, *The Citizen* became a tabloid. (*A History of the County of Gloucester, Volume IV: The City of Gloucester*, ed. N.M. Herbert, 1988; *The Citizen*)

MAY 2ND

1889: The Royal Albert Theatre had a packed house on this night, for the first ever performance in Gloucester of Gilbert and Sullivan's *Yeoman of the Guard*. The popular duo's latest work had been put on at Cheltenham a few months previously, but for many of the Gloucester audience, this was the first time that they had seen or heard the light opera, although its fame had preceded it to every town and city in the British Isles.

In the cast of this particular production were some artists who had played at Gloucester before, and they were given a hearty welcome. Cairns James played Jack Point, the strolling jester, and Miss Jessie Moore was Elsie Maynard. The part of Wilfred Shadbolt was cleverly performed by Edward Clowes, and Miss Kate Foster was an excellent Phoebe Meryll. Miss Kate Talby was Dame Carruthers, and Miss Rose Von Waldeck played her niece. In the opinion of the local press, the whole opera was produced admirably, the principals were good and the chorus was a well-balanced one. A special word of praise was given to the conductor, and sometimes member of the orchestra, Mr Mozart Wilson. (*The Citizen*)

MAY 3RD

1471: In this year, the deposed Lancastrian king, Henry VI, died; an event which resulted in another outbreak of fighting in the War of the Roses. Henry's widow, Margaret of Anjou, journeyed from France to England, supported by the army of the Duke of Somerset, to fight for the claim of her and Henry's son, Edward, to be king in place of the Yorkist Edward IV. Margaret's party landed in Weymouth in April, and made its way north, arriving in Bristol on May 1st. The Lancastrians wanted to rendezvous with supporters in Wales, which meant crossing the River Severn, and the nearest place to do this was at Gloucester. King Edward heard of Margaret's intention to go to Gloucester, and sent an order to the Governor there to hold out against the Queen and Somerset for as long as possible.

The Lancastrians arrived outside the city at 10 o'clock in the morning on May 3rd, to find the gates closed against them. Knowing King Edward was near, Margaret did not have time to fight, so she carried on towards Tewkesbury, arriving there with her exhausted troops on the night of May 3rd. On the next day, Edward's army engaged with hers in battle. The Lancastrians were defeated, Margaret captured, and her son killed. (Hammond, P.W., *The Battles of Barnet and Tewkesbury*, 1990)

MAY 4TH

1895: The Gloucester Harriers held an athletic meeting at Kingsholm. There were only two events in the programme, but nearly sixty entries had been received, including 'the cream of the long-distance athletes'. The weather was good, but only about 500 or 600 spectators attended.

The first event was the 220 Yards Open Handicap. There were five heats, and the winner of each went into the final. W.J. Matthews of Stroud Harriers came first in the final, and won five guineas. The second event was the Ten Miles Open Flat Handicap, with a first prize of the President's Cup and ten guineas. A gold medal would also be awarded to the first Gloucester Harrier to finish. For this race, twenty-four entries had been received, but only about half of the athletes turned up, and those missing included many of the best racers. Several of the Birchfield Harriers would have been present, if not for the fact that they missed their train at Birmingham. W.H. Harrison of Shrewsbury Harriers came first, in a time of 54 minutes and 15 seconds. C.W. Giles of Gloucester Harriers came fourth, and was presented with the medal for the first member of the host club to finish. An objection was lodged against the winner for entering in the wrong name, but this came to nothing. (*The Citizen*)

MAY 5TH

1902: John Bellows, printer of Gloucester, died. On the same day, *The Citizen* printed a lengthy obituary. Bellows was born in Liskeard, Cornwall, in 1831. He served an apprenticeship with a printer, then worked for a while in London, before moving to Gloucester. He managed a printing office in Westgate Street for a number of years before setting up his own printing business. As well as running this, he found the time to produce the first ever French-English pocket dictionary.

Bellows was a Quaker, an Elder of the Gloucester Meeting, who kept to the traditional way of dressing (always wearing his wide-brimmed black hat) and speaking. He was an enthusiastic archaeologist and member of the Bristol and Gloucestershire Archaeological Society. In 1872, when he was building new business premises in Eastgate Street, he discovered the Roman wall of Gloucester, in what was then the garden of Eastgate House. He was also a member of the Cotteswold Naturalists Field Club.

Bellows had been in poor health for some time, since returning with his wife from a trip to America, where he had received an honorary Masters degree from Harvard University. He died in his home of nearly twenty years, Upton Knoll, in Upton St Leonards. (*The Citizen*)

MAY 6TH

1322: Sir John Giffard of Brimpsfield was one of the barons who had risen up against Edward II and his favourites, the Despensers. In 1321, after disturbances in the Marches, Giffard was ordered to attend a meeting of the Magnates to be held at Gloucester on April 5th, but he failed to appear. In December of that year, he was declared to be an enemy of the King. Edward II spent Christmas at Cirencester, not far from Brimpsfield. While at Cirencester, he ordered Brimpsfield Castle to be levelled, and all other Giffard property be taken into custody. In retaliation, Sir John attacked the royal baggage train as it passed near Brimpsfield. He was captured in 1322 in Yorkshire, at the Battle of Boroughbridge, and was taken to Pontefract Castle. On May 6th, he was tried at Gloucester and found guilty of high treason. He was executed on the same day. (Butler, R.F., 'The Last of the Brimpsfield Giffords and the Rising of 1321-22', in *Transactions of the Bristol and Gloucestershire Archaeological Society*, Volume 76)

MAY 7TH

1932: In the regular column entitled 'Gloucester Notes' in the *Cheltenham Chronicle*, the writer stated that the damage being done in the city by youths and small boys had reached a degree previously unknown to the police. Windows were broken daily around the docks, and often more serious damage was done. A difficulty was presented by the fact that when the offenders were caught, their parents had to pay the bill, and as they were usually of poorer families, magistrates were reluctant to impose sharp fines. The remedy was, the author of the piece believed, corporal punishment, which would probably serve as a deterrent to the youngsters, who were often beyond the control of their parents.

It was not only property-owners who suffered at their hands, the article went on. Motorists who parked their cars in the official stands returned to find children climbing all over them. In the evening, they chased helter-skelter round the arcades of shops, and throughout the school holidays did this during the day too. Urchins pestered people for money, or irritated them in many other ways. The traders of the city needed to make a formal protest, because the present state of affairs was no advertisement for shopping in Gloucester. (*Cheltenham Chronicle*)

MAY 8TH

1943: 'Wings for Victory' week began in Gloucester, organised by the National Savings Committee. This was a fund-raising event, encouraging citizens to invest in Government saving schemes such as War Bonds and Savings Certificates. The money was then borrowed by the Government to buy war equipment, in this case bombers. Gloucester had set itself a target of making £1 million, in order to enable the Government to buy twenty Lancasters and forty Typhoons.

The opening ceremony was preceded by a parade of over 2,000 people, representing the Army, the Navy and the Air Force, the United States Forces, Civil Defence Forces, Sea Cadets, Army Cadet Corps, Girls' Training Corps, Women's Land Army, Girl Guides, Sea Rangers and Boy Scouts. The salute was taken by the Duke of Beaufort, Lord Lieutenant of the County and Lord High Steward of the City. A week later, it was announced that Gloucester and district had managed to raise a total of £1,012,718. (*Gloucester Journal*)

MAY 9TH

1901: A meeting of Gloucester hairdressers was held at Worcester Street Coffee House. At this time, hairdressers and their clients were all men. Mr Abel Evans presided. He told the meeting that hairdressers in the city were labouring under bad conditions, with regard to the pay they received. The prices of materials had gone up, as had house and shop rents. In Gloucester, thirty-four hairdressers were engaged in the trade, serving a population of about 47,000, and when they took from that number the female population, those who went to the aristocratic shops, those who tried to shave themselves, and those who never came for a haircut, the margin for hairdressers to exist upon was very much narrowed down. Evans believed that it would be a good idea to form an association, which would agree on prices.

The meeting agreed that the price of haircutting should be raised to 3 pence, shaving to 1½ pence, and haircutting of school-age children to 2 pence. Four visitors from the Cheltenham Hairdressers' Association then explained how their association worked. Subsequently, the meeting resolved to form the Gloucester Hairdressers' Association, and officers and a committee were elected. (*The Citizen*)

MAY 10TH

1878: Early in the morning, between midnight and one o'clock, Police Constables Seats and Child were on patrol in the neighbourhood of Quedgeley House, when they met a couple of suspicious-looking men. Asked what they were doing and where they were going, the men replied that they were sailors and were returning from Stroud to their ship. The constables were not satisfied, so they followed the men and again questioned them. At this point, one of them drew a pistol and fired twice. The shot aimed at PC Child missed, but PC Seats was hit in the knee. The men ran away and Child called for assistance, then took his colleague to the Infirmary. At the Gloucester Assizes in August, Samuel Ellis (alias George Fragley, alias Deaf George), was sentenced to life imprisonment for feloniously wounding PC Seats. (*The Citizen*)

MAY 11TH

1815: At the Theatre Royal, an amateur performance was put on before a very large audience of fashionable people. The play was *Julius Caesar*, and the part of Brutus was played by Colonel Berkeley. He was joined by John Austin, who played Cassius, Captain Augustus Berkeley, who was Mark Antony, and Captain Probyn, who took the role of Metellus. The other parts were played by regular performers. All the amateurs gave creditable performances, and the play was well received by the audience. (*Morning Post*)

———◆———

1932: A new Marks & Spencer store opened in Northgate Street. The company had first come to Gloucester some time before 1912, when it opened a Penny Bazaar in Southgate Street. In 1913, a move was made to No. 8 Northgate Street, where the store stayed for nearly thirty years, before moving into bigger premises at No. 17 Northgate Street, in 1932. In 1936, the shop next door became available, and Marks & Spencer took the opportunity to expand its premises. In 2012, Marks & Spencer moved into the former Woolworths store in Eastgate Street. (Voyce, J., *The City of Gloucester*, 1995; www. marksintime.marksandspencer.com)

MAY 12TH

1942: At an annual meeting of Gloucester Freemen, a resolution was passed agreeing to surrender their ancient rights to graze their animals on the Archdeacon and Meanham Meadows, in exchange for a payment of £625 compensation from the Gloucester Corporation. (*Gloucester Journal*)

———— • ◆ • ————

1972: King's Square was officially opened by Peter Walker, the Secretary of State for the Environment. The new shopping centre contained fifty-eight shop units, a supermarket, a restaurant and office accommodation. Filling the middle of the square was a large water feature, with fountains and concrete stepping stones. Servicing to the shops and offices was at the first-floor level, so that the square could be completely vehicle-free. There was a multi-storey car park next to the development, and there was a subway link to the bus station. The motto of the new enterprise was 'King's Square – a new heart for the city'.

Mr Walker pressed a button which turned on the fountains, accompanied by a fanfare of trumpets. He congratulated the city on the project, and commented that Gloucester had been given a new vigour and elegance. The Minister then unveiled a plaque in honour of the occasion, watched by Geoffrey Jellicoe, the planning consultant whose 1961 plan for the city included the layout of the square. Mr Jellicoe said afterwards that he was absolutely delighted with the results of his scheme. (*The Citizen*)

MAY 13TH

1926: The General Strike in Britain had started on May 4th. Many workers in Gloucester joined in, affecting the railways and the newspapers. At the docks, there had been trouble between strikers and employers, and, on this day, the bad feeling escalated into violence. The trouble began when the owners of a tug decided to send it, and an empty lighter, along the canal to Sharpness to pick up a cargo, and a union member agreed to sail with a crew of volunteers. A crowd of dockers and seamen gathered and the union man decided against manning the tug and left, but the volunteer crew tried to leave the dock, assisted by police on board. Struggles broke out between the pickets and the police at the swing bridges. It took a baton charge before the dockers fell back and the tug could continue on its journey. Fourteen men were arrested as a result of the disturbance. (Williams, A.R., 'The General Strike in Gloucestershire', in *Transactions of the Bristol and Gloucestershire Archaeological Society*, Volume 91)

MAY 14TH

1903: A notice in *The Citizen* announced that the Annual Conference of Women Workers of Great Britain and Ireland would be held in Gloucester and Cheltenham in November. A preliminary meeting of the local branch was to be held at the Glevum Hall in Southgate Street, on May 27th, when Miss Clifford of Bristol would speak on 'MAKING THE MOST OF LIFE'. Anyone interested in women's work was invited to attend, and admission was free. (*The Citizen*)

———•◆•———

1895: An inquest was held at the Infirmary, on Arthur Miller, aged 15, who had died in the hospital as a result of injuries he received in a crane accident. Miller was employed on a longboat, and was helping to unload a cargo of iron bars at the Gloucester Railway Carriages and Wagon Company's wharf on the canal. The crew used a crane belonging to the company, which was a portable one, having wheels and a balance-box. The crane was lifting some bars when its arm suddenly swung the wrong way, and the balance-box toppled over and fell on Arthur Miller. He was taken to the Infirmary, where he was found to have suffered multiple fractures, and died that night. The jury returned a verdict of accidental death, with no blame being attached to anyone. (*The Citizen*)

MAY 15TH

1885: A prominent Gloucester couple, Mr and Mrs Jesse Sessions, celebrated their golden wedding anniversary. By coincidence, the day of the week on which their anniversary fell was the same as the day on which they married – a Friday. Few ladies would get married on this day, believing it to be unlucky, but the long marriage of this couple showed that this was a superstition without substance.

Alderman Sessions had invited about seventy of their friends to a tea, which was held at the Raikes Memorial School in Brunswick Road. The schoolroom had been draped with curtains and made to look as much as possible like a drawing room. After tea, Mr J.J. Seekings rose to congratulate the couple, hoping that they would enjoy many more years together. Mr Sessions returned thanks, and said that though fifty years of marriage must naturally bring its share of trials and perplexities, he had never disagreed with his wife so far as to fall out with her. Several of the temperance societies then gave addresses. Mr Sessions said that he had been involved in temperance work for fifty-three years and he believed he was the only one left of those who formed the Gloucester Temperance Society in 1833. Mrs Sessions also thanked the deputations. The golden wedding cake was then cut and distributed. (*The Citizen*)

MAY 16TH

1907: R.A. Lister & Co. Ltd of Station Road, Gloucester, advertised its lawnmower repair service. Blades could be sharpened using their new power grinder, which would make the cutting knives as good as new. Machines could be fetched from and delivered to customers in Gloucester. Listers also sold new mowers, with a variety of makes in stock including Rensome's, Green's, Pennsylvania, and Clippers, stocked in large quantities and supplied at short notice. Prices started at 12s 6d. (*The Citizen*)

1936: A rally of Girl Guides was held in Gloucester, in which over 2,000 girls took part. The Princess Royal was supposed to be attending, but was unable to come because of illness, so her place was taken by her cousin, the Duchess of Beaufort, who was the County President of the movement. The rally took place on the Kingsholm Rugby Ground. Many prominent city and council people were present and watched a programme of physical exercises, historical pageantry, demonstrations of various kinds, the construction of a model camp and a variety of camping activities. The massing of all the county companies in their familiar uniforms was a spectacular sight. About 200 Brownies also joined in the proceedings. (*Cheltenham Chronicle*)

May 17th

1837: This was a busy day at the Gloucester Petty Sessions:

- John Dowding, Eliza Dowding and Ann Langley were charged with assaulting Police Constables Nos 8 and 13. John Dowding was fined 10 shillings and Ann Langley 5 shillings (both including costs), but the case against Eliza Dowding was dismissed, not being proved.
- George White made a complaint against Ann, the wife of William Moore, for assaulting him. The case was dismissed.
- George Harris, a policeman, accused Hester, the wife of George Hipwood, of assaulting him in the execution of his duty. Hester Hipwood was fined 10 shillings, including costs.
- Eliza, the wife of Thomas Crouch, made a complaint against Elizabeth, the wife of John Reames, for an assault. The defendant was ordered to pay costs.
- Harriet Lee, the wife of William Lee, complained of John Lee, for an assault. John Lee was fined 1 shilling, or he could spend 24 hours in prison.

(Gloucestershire Archives, Gloucester Borough Records, GBR/G4/M1/1)

MAY 18TH

1893: A pigeon-shooting match was held at the Llanthony ground at Hempsted. The competitors included the best shots in the West of England, who took part under assumed names. A number of 10 shilling sweepstakes were held in the morning. After lunch, the event of the day was a £1 sweepstake for a £50 purse. This was divided between Messrs Allen, Davis, Graham, and Ellicott, who all killed their five birds.

Next came the £1 sweepstakes, won by Messrs Allen, Smith, Ellicott, Graham and Chamberlain. 'Double rises', in which honours were equally divided, ended an extremely pleasant day for the participants. Mr Heath of the Raglan Arms Hotel organised the event, which was the first to be held in Gloucester for many years. Mr Williams of Cinderford supplied the birds, which were said to be 'remarkably good and strong on the wing'. (*The Citizen*)

May 19th

1900: The news of the relief of Mafeking in South Africa had reached Britain, and celebrations took place nationwide. In Gloucester, thousands of people gathered in the Park to take part in a demonstration organised by the Mayor. There was music by the Civic Military Band, a lantern exhibition and illuminations, and a display of fireworks. The band came prepared with an ambitious programme of music, but the crowd only wanted to hear *Soldiers of the Queen*, *Tommy Atkins* and *Rule Britannia*.

Photographic war slides were shown by Mr Smart, and when the pictures of Generals were shown on screen, the crowd cheered loudly. Photographs of the Hero of Mafeking (Colonel Baden-Powell) were the most popular, and *See the Conquering Hero Comes* was played as an accompaniment. After the fireworks, the Mayor gave a speech, recalling that for seven long months Baden-Powell and his men had been confined in Mafeking, assailed on all sides by the Boers, and rejoiced that at last the British Forces had rescued them. (*The Citizen*)

1881: The following notice appeared in *The Citizen*:

GARDEN ROLL – Missing from the Bowling Green at the Spa, a Stone Garden-roll, iron-mounted; any person having removed the same is requested at once to replace it. If detained after this notice legal proceedings will be taken.

MAY 20TH

1890: An inquest was held by the City Coroner to enquire into the death of William Harris, of Percy Street, Tredworth, who had died as the result of a serious accident in the gymnasium at Tynedale Schoolroom, Gloucester. Benjamin Harris, brother of the deceased, said William was 17 years old and a blacksmith. He was a member of Tynedale Athletic Club and had gone to the schoolroom in the evening for gym practice. He saw his brother on the trapeze, about 6 or 7 feet off the ground, not performing, but just sitting on it. Benjamin was talking to some friends when he heard a thud, and turned round and saw his brother on the floor. They laid William on a mattress and asked him what had happened. He said he was sitting on the bar of the trapeze, but didn't remember anything else until his head hit the floor.

A juryman asked the brother if it was not usual practice to place a mat under the trapeze, and he replied that there would have been a mat if someone had been performing. A house surgeon at the Infirmary said the deceased had a fractured spine and died eight days after the accident. The immediate cause of death was spinal meningitis, caused by the injuries he had received. The jury returned a verdict of accidental death. (*The Citizen*)

MAY 21ST

1946: At a crowded meeting held in the Guildhall, the constitution of the newly-formed Gloucester City Community Council was unanimously approved. This was the Community Council's first annual meeting, and about sixty bodies and organisations which would be co-operating in its work were represented. It was agreed that one of the main aims of the Council would be to promote the wellbeing of the community, by making a common effort to further health, to advance education, to provide a meeting place and facilities for physical and mental training and recreation, to promote social, moral and intellectual improvement, and to foster a community spirit for the achievement of these purposes. The Council wanted to establish a People's House in the city to provide for the central needs of the community, and also to assist in the opening of community centres in the new areas of the city. The constitution had already been approved by the National Council of Social Service, to which the Gloucester Community Council would be affiliated. (*Gloucester Journal*)

1879: A notice in the local press announced that Maccabe, 'a wonderful impersonator, ventriloquist and mimic', was appearing at the Corn Exchange that evening, for the first performance in a two-night visit to Gloucester. He was to begin his show with the celebrated entertainment, *Begone, dull care*, which had drawn large crowds in London, Philadelphia, and other large towns. (*The Citizen*)

MAY 22ND

1966: Thomas William John Goddard, the Gloucestershire and England cricketer, died at the age of 65. Born in Gloucester in 1900, he joined Gloucestershire in 1922 as a fast bowler. In 1928, his contract was not renewed and he joined the ground staff at Lords, where he started to experiment with spin-bowling. Finding that Goddard had a new talent, Gloucestershire re-engaged him for the 1929 season, and his success as an off-spinner led to a call-up for the England team. He played for England eight times. After his retirement, at the end of the 1952 season, Goddard opened a furniture shop in Barton Street, which he ran until a year before his death. (*Wisden Cricketers' Almanack*)

1893: This was Whit Monday, and a fête and military tournament was held on the Kingsholm Athletic Ground, organised by the Ancient Order of Foresters. There were displays by the 12th Lancers, and the programme included sword exercises, lemon cutting, tent pegging, a Victoria Cross Race, and other competitions. The Band of the 1st Gloucestershire Volunteer Royal Engineers attended, and a string band played to accompany dancing. Another feature was the Ashley team of American skaters who gave performances, and there was a Punch and Judy show. In the evening, there was a grand display of fireworks. (*The Citizen*)

MAY 23RD

1768: A notice appeared in the *Gloucester Journal*, asking that anyone sending patients to the Gloucester Infirmary should take care that they were sent 'clean and free from vermin', and had a proper changes of clothes, namely three shirts or three shifts, and other necessities for keeping them clean. (*Gloucester Journal*)

1907: The annual meeting of the Gloucester Branch of the English Church Union was held at St Aldate's Schoolroom. The Secretary read out the annual report, and told those present that since the last annual meeting, four associate members had left the district and one membership had lapsed, while two members had died. On the other hand, thirty-six new members, associate members and women associates had been introduced. The election of officers then took place, and Mr R. Groves Morris was unanimously re-elected as Chairman.

The Chairman announced that he wanted to introduce something new to their meetings, which was the singing of a good fighting hymn, *The Faith of Our Forefathers*. That was what they wanted – the faith of their forefathers. They wanted enthusiasm. There was no enthusiasm in Gloucester in religious matters. There was plenty of enthusiasm in football and politics, but not in religion. The hymn was then sung, to the Chairman's accompaniment. (*The Citizen*)

MAY 24TH

1893: The old custom of the Gloucester Corporation sending a lamprey pie to the monarch was revived by the mayor, Mr Matthews, who on this day personally delivered the delicacy to Buckingham Palace, to mark the occasion of Queen Victoria's birthday. From medieval times, Gloucester had sent a lamprey pie to the reigning king or queen at Christmas, but this was an expensive practice, especially at that time of year, and the tradition was ended before Victoria became queen. The lamprey pie was made by John Ambrose Fisher of Tudor House, Westgate Street. It was elaborately decorated and was accompanied by a pair of 'skewers', or spoons, bearing the arms of the City and the name of the Mayor. Fisher continued to make a lamprey pie for the sovereign every year from then, until his retirement.

Although the annual custom of baking a lamprey pie died out, they are occasionally still prepared for special royal occasions. It was decided to make one to celebrate Queen Elizabeth's Diamond Jubilee in 2012, but as lampreys were now a protected species in the river Severn, the pie's main ingredient had to be brought in from Canada. (*The Citizen*)

———•◆•———

1879: Horse-drawn trams began to run in Gloucester, after the route was passed by an Inspector. The fare was two pence, for a part or a full journey. (*Gloucester Journal*)

MAY 25TH

1136: The church at Llanthony Priory Secunda in Gloucester was founded on this day. The church took about sixteen months to build, and was dedicated on September 10th 1137. It was built using money the canons had saved from their original priory in Wales, supplemented by gifts from the Bishop of Hereford, who granted Llanthony the churches of Prestbury and Sevenhampton. ('Priors of Llanthony By Gloucester', by J.N. Langton, *Transactions of the Bristol and Gloucestershire Archaeological Society*, Volume 63)

———◆———

1927: A Bohemian Dance took place at the Palais de Danse in George Street, organised by 'Uncle and Co.' About 120 people attended, a large number of whom took advantage of the option to appear in flannels. A varied programme of dances was enjoyed, and the event went on until half past one in the morning. The music was provided by Mr Billy Burgess's band. (*The Citizen*)

May 26th

1804: An advertisement appeared in *The Times* for 'a spacious and elegant new-built mansion situated at Barnwood, near Gloucester', which was available to be let immediately. The house consisted of a dining room, which was 26 feet long and 18 feet wide, a drawing room of similar dimensions, a breakfast parlour, housekeeper's rooms, a servants' hall and kitchen, eight airy and large bedrooms with dressing rooms and closets, servants' bedrooms, a laundry, a coach-house, stables, etc. Outside were pleasure and kitchen gardens and about five acres of pasture land, with more available if required. The drawing room, dining room and bedrooms were fitted with 'elegant marble pieces', stoves and grates. Barnwood was described as being 'a remarkably pleasant and healthy village'. Post-paid applications were to be made to Messrs Read and Son, Auctioneers, of Gloucester.

The house was built by Robert Morris, a banker and MP for Gloucester from 1805 to 1816, who lived in nearby Barnwood Court. It was bought in about 1808 by Sir Charles Hotham. In 1860 it was converted and extended to become a mental hospital for private patients. (*The Times*; 'Barnwood House and Grounds', by H. and R. Conway Jones, *Gloucestershire History*, 2004)

MAY 27TH

1885: At the City Petty Sessions, Robert Baker, aged 15, was charged with stealing a flower. Police Constable Gobey stated that he met the prisoner late at night, and thinking he had something concealed under his coat, challenged him. The boy produced a tulip, which he said he had taken from a garden in Falkner Street. The constable went there and found a tulip bulb lying on the flowerbed, with a broken stalk.

The Revd P.J. Cocking, owner of the tulip, said the boy had no right to take the flower out of his garden, and that he appeared against him in recognition of police efforts to put a stop to these thefts, not on account of the value of the flower. Baker's employer gave him a good character reference. He was fined 2s 6d and costs, plus damages of 6d. The Revd L.A. Lyne of All Saints paid the fine. He said he knew that the boy had lost his mother when he was three years old, and he had been much neglected. The Revd Cocking gave Baker the 6d he had received in damages, towards the payment of his expenses. (*The Citizen*)

MAY 28TH

1234: For years, King Henry III had been embroiled in a fight with rebellious barons. In 1232, Hubert de Burgh, a powerful lord from the Welsh Marshes and the ex-justicier of England, was accused of high treason. He was imprisoned for a time in Devizes, but managed to escape to Wales, where he joined forces with Henry's enemy, Llewelyn, the Welsh prince. Hubert was joined there by other rebellious lords.

In 1234, King Henry journeyed to Gloucester to meet with the Archbishop of Canterbury and other Bishops, who had negotiated an agreement with Llewelyn. The Archbishop told Henry that as part of the agreement, he must be reconciled with the noblemen who had allied themselves with Llewelyn. Wanting peace at any price, Henry agreed, and summoned the exiled lords, assuring them that they would have safe conduct, and would receive a full pardon and have their forfeited estates returned to them. On this day, the nobles, including Hubert de Burgh, obeyed the summons and came to Gloucester, where the King received them with the kiss or peace. (*Anglo-Saxon Chronicles*)

MAY 29TH

1785: Elizabeth Lander and Mary Southern, wife of Thomas Southern, both from Gloucester, appeared before a justice of the peace, charged with cutting and stealing cabbages from the garden of James Holbert, a gardener of Kingsholm. John Smith, a labourer of Kingsholm, appeared as a witness against them. No verdict was recorded. (*Calendar of Summary Convictions at Petty Sessions, 1781-1837*, ed. I. Wyatt, Gloucestershire Record Series, Volume 22, 2008)

———◆———

1864: A lady attended Sunday service at the Cathedral dressed in the latest fashion – a crinoline. As she was leaving the pew at the end of the service, a large hassock got stuck up her skirts and would not budge, no matter how much she wriggled, twisted and shook. Eventually, one of the lay clerks came to the lady's assistance, and managed to free her by lifting her skirts gently, one at a time, until he found and removed the offending item. (*Western Daily Press*)

MAY 30TH

1892: The anniversary dinner of the Royal Gloucester Lodge (No. 96) of the Ancient Order of Druids (a fraternal organisation) took place at the Ram Hotel, where sixty-two brethren and friends sat down to an excellent meal. After the cloth had been removed, the Chairman read out apologies from members who had been unable to attend, and proposed the toasts to the Queen and the Royal Family, which were duly honoured, and the National Anthem was sung.

In the absence of the Mayor, Mr R.J. Talbot gave the toast of 'The Ancient Order of Druids, and Lodge No.96', wishing the Order every prosperity. Brother F. Andrews said that although the Order was not one of the largest or wealthiest in the country, it was of great antiquity, because even before the Christian era, the Druids were playing an important role in the social and religious life of this and other countries. During the evening, songs were sung by a number of brothers and guests, accompanied by Mr W.H. Morgan, presiding on the piano. (*The Citizen*)

MAY 31ST

1900: Gloucester Public Library in Brunswick Road was formally opened. The streets had been decorated with bunting for the occasion, which began with the Mayor and Corporation making its way in procession from the Guildhall to Brunswick Road. The library was opened by Lord Avebury, who said in his speech that, now there was a place in the city holding so many treasures, 'no-one in Gloucester need ever be dull again'. This assertion was greeted by loud applause. At the main entrance, Lord Avebury formally unlocked the door and declared the Library open to the public. At the suggestion of the Mayor, a verse of the National Anthem was sung, followed by three hearty cheers. (*The Citizen*)

———— ◆ ————

1887: The funeral was held at Gloucester cemetery of the two daughters of Alderman Knowles – Mrs Kate Summers and Miss Minnie Knowles, who had died in a fire at the *Opera Comique* in Paris, which had killed or injured over 200 people. Great sympathy was shown to the family in the city, with hundreds of people lining the route as the funeral procession made its way to the cemetery, and tradesmen closing their shops for the duration of the service. The funeral was attended by the Mayor and the High Sheriff, on behalf of the Corporation. Mrs Summers and Miss Knowles were interred in the family vault, where their mother already lay. (*The Citizen*)

JUNE 1st

1866: Two sunburnt soldiers of the 62nd Regiment told an extraordinary tale to the Gloucester Magistrates on this day. James Smith and John Hall said that on May 24th, they had been strolling on the beach at Portland, where their detachment was stationed, when the cap of one of them was blown off and into the sea. In trying to recover it, he fell into the water and couldn't get out, so his companion got into a nearby boat and rescued him. Unfortunately, the boat only had one oar, so they were unable to get it back to the beach, and were carried out into the ocean. They drifted all that night, the next day and the following night, with nothing to eat or drink.

On the day after that, David Pershand, captain of a Jersey cutter which was making for the port of Gloucester, spied their red jackets and brass buttons glittering in the sun, about 55 miles off Portland. He managed to get out to them and take them on board his vessel. He gave the men food and drink and brought them to Gloucester, which they had reached the day before. No specific charge was made against them, but they were ordered to be detained in custody until their commanding officer at Gosport had been communicated with. (*The Citizen*)

JUNE 2ND

1941: The Cheese Rolling event at Coopers Hill, Brockworth, was held as usual on Whit Monday this year, but for the first time within memory the event took place without a cheese. Because of the food shortage during the war, the key ingredient of the competition was substituted by wooden dummies. These wooden 'cheeses' were rolled down the steep slope, and as usual, there was a great scramble of people chasing after them, but the winners had to be content with money prizes.

The annual Wake attracted a large attendance, and there was almost as much excitement as usual when the Master of Ceremonies, in his smock and ribbons, gave the signal for each 'cheese' to be rolled. There were other events as well as the cheese rolling, including foot races, and a tug-of-war. (*Western Daily Press*)

JUNE 3RD

1871: The foundation stone was laid in Brunswick Road by the County Sheriff, William Playne, of a new building which was intended to hold a permanent museum, a school of art, and a school of science. An initial meeting had been called in April 1870, of gentlemen interested in establishing such an institution. Thomas Gambier Parry was elected joint secretary of the committee with G.F. Riddiford.

The task of raising subscriptions began, and the site in Brunswick Road was chosen. Designs were published later that month, showing the museum and science school on the ground floor and an art school upstairs. Eventually, money was raised by subscription, and the building was opened on April 15th 1873, by Lord Ducie. (Rhodes, J., 'Gambier Parry and Gloucester Schools of Art and Science', in *Transactions of the Bristol and Gloucestershire Archaeological Society*, Volume 118)

JUNE 4TH

1895: This was the second day of the Kingsholm Fête, arranged by Fred McCrea, on behalf of the Gloucester Football and Athletic Ground Company. On both evenings, the highlight of the entertainment was provided by Professor Gaudron making an ascent in a hot air balloon and a descent in a parachute. The first night's performance had gone without any problem, and on this evening, Gaudron went up in the balloon as before, then jumped out and opened his parachute, landing safely in a garden near St Catherine's Church. The balloon, however, relieved of the weight of its passenger, carried on climbing until it was lost from sight among the clouds. It was supposed to have collapsed after Gaudron left it, but he had forgotten to put the customary weight on top of the balloon before he jumped. It was reported that the balloon came down in Quedgeley, landing in a clover field. A man was sent in a cab to collect it the next morning. (*The Citizen*)

JUNE 5TH

1873: An opening ceremony was held for the unveiling of the new reredos at Gloucester Cathedral, made by the masons of the province, and paid for by the Freemasons of Gloucestershire. Designed by Gilbert Scott, the reredos (an ornamental screen) was 17 feet 6 inches wide. Statues in its niches depicted Moses bearing the tablets of law, the Nativity, St Peter, The Ascension, St Paul, The Entombment of the Saviour, and David bearing the harp.

The occasion began with the holding of a Grand Provincial Lodge, led by the Provincial Grand Master, Lord Sherborne. At three o'clock, a procession, led by the Mayor and Corporation, made its way to the Cathedral, where it was met by the Bishop in his full scarlet canonicals and doctor's hood. A curtain was slowly opened to reveal the reredos, which was then formally presented by the Grand Master to the church dignitaries. The choir then sang the *Hallelujah Chorus*. That evening, a Masonic banquet was held at the Bell Hotel, attended by nearly 150 brethren. (*The Graphic*)

JUNE 6TH

1791: This day saw the opening of the new Theatre Royal in Westgate Street, owned by Mr Watson, who was also the proprietor of the theatre at Cheltenham. Although the building work was not quite finished, as the plastering still had to be done, Watson opened the theatre for six days, for a production of Shakespeare's *As You Like It*. The building then closed for the work to be completed, with the intention of opening properly for the winter season. (*Gloucester Journal*)

1927: The annual Gloucester Lawn Tennis Tournament began, on the private courts of Mr A. Hudson, at Longford. Competitors who took part in the event came from Cirencester, Cheltenham, Tewkesbury and Ross, as well as Gloucester. The tournament carried on into the following day, but had to be curtailed because of rain. (*The Citizen*)

JUNE 7TH

1879: An inquest was held at Mr Gleed's house in Bristol Road, into the death of 62-year-old Thomas Jones, an excavator of Little Norwood Street. Jones had been badly injured in an accident at the Gas Works in Hempsted, where men were making excavations for a new tank. The earth had to be dug out to a considerable depth, and Jones was inside the hole with another worker named Harris when one side of the excavation collapsed and buried them. Their workmates removed the soil as quickly as possible, and Harris was brought out alive, but badly injured; Jones was found to be dead when he was pulled out of the earth. A verdict of accidental death was returned. (*The Citizen*)

———— • ◆ • ————

1939: The last man to be executed in Gloucester died on this day. Ralph Smith was hanged inside the prison, having been found guilty of killing his former landlady in Swindon. The executioner was Thomas Pierrepoint. (Evans, J., *Hanged at Gloucester*, 2011)

JUNE 8TH

1898: An appalling accident took place on the Gloucester Docks Railway, late at night. An engine driver and three other workers were in charge of a goods train, consisting of twenty-seven wagons, loaded with timber and other materials. As the engine crossed over the points connecting a siding with the main line, it jumped the metals and part of the train left the track. The line ran alongside the Gloucester & Berkeley Canal, and the men feared the engine would topple into the water, so they jumped down.

The engine driver landed on his feet and was able to avoid the approaching trucks, but the other three fell more awkwardly and were hit by the wagons. The foreman shunter, who was pinned under the trucks, was killed almost instantly. Another shunter had his right leg torn off and his other leg was badly crushed. The other worker, a driver, suffered fractures of his right thigh bone and his collarbone. Both of these men were taken to the Infirmary, but died within a few hours. Three days later, a carter was killed on the same railway after being knocked down by a train. (*The Citizen*)

JUNE 9TH

1611: On this day, Giles Thomson was consecrated as Bishop of Gloucester. He died on June 14th 1612, never having visited his see. (*Fasti Ecclesiae Anglicanae, 1541-1837*, ed. J.M. Horn, Volume 8, 1996)

———◆———

1882: At the City Petty Sessions, Elizabeth Pugh was charged with assaulting Mary Sheppard. The complainant said that the two had got involved in an argument in Ducie Street, and some words were exchanged, before the defendant hit her with a bucket. Sheppard's mother said that she saw the two women, who were sisters-in-law, on the ground fighting. She did not see who struck the first blow.

Mary Sheppard, Caroline Pugh and Matilda Hyam were then charged with assaulting Elizabeth Pugh. The complainant said as soon as her husband left the house, the three women started using bad language towards her. She retreated into her house, and Mary Sheppard came in and dragged her out by her hair. All three women then pounced on her. She denied hitting Mary Sheppard with the bucket.

A witness said Sheppard dragged Elizabeth Pugh out of the house by the hair, then the other two women had tried to separate them. The case against Caroline Pugh, Matilda Hyam and Elizabeth Pugh was dismissed, and Mary Sheppard was fined 2 shillings and costs, or seven days imprisonment. She elected to go to prison. (*The Citizen*)

JUNE 10TH

1675: Jane Burgess of Littleworth appeared in the Gloucester Consistory Court to accuse the rector of St Mary de Crypt, Richard Littleton, of fathering her daughter Elizabeth's illegitimate child. Evidence was given over the following four weeks, from which it transpired that in the summer of 1674, Elizabeth Burgess had several meetings with Littleton at an alehouse in Barnwood. By January of the next year, it became obvious that Elizabeth was pregnant, and when questioned, she named Littleton as the father. She gave birth to a boy on March 16th, who died two days later.

After the witnesses against Littleton had been heard, a host of influential men appeared in court in support of the clergyman. However, it was clear that Littleton had a reputation for keeping company with young women of a lower social position than himself. He had appeared before the Church Court before, in 1668, because of his drunken and licentious behaviour. No verdict of the court was given in the records, but Littleton was replaced as the rector of St Mary de Crypt in the summer of 1675. He was also rector of Longney parish, and he remained as minister there up to his death in 1715. (Ripley, P., 'A Seventeenth-Century Consistory Court Case', in *Transactions of the Bristol and Gloucestershire Archaeological Society*, Volume 100)

JUNE 11TH

1931: Princess Mary visited Gloucester to lay the foundation stone of the new wing of the Royal Infirmary. She arrived from London in a special saloon at the Great Western Railway station, which was bedecked with flags. The Duke and Duchess of Beaufort and the Dowager Duchess of Beaufort were among those who met Her Royal Highness. (*Bath Chronicle*)

———— • ◆ • ————

1907: The second day of a county cricket match between Gloucestershire and Northamptonshire took place at the Spa. At the close of play the day before, the home team had scored 20 runs and had lost 4 wickets. On this day, Gloucestershire were all out for 60. This seemed embarrassing, but Northants were then bowled out for 12 runs. Gloucestershire recovered some pride in their second innings, managing to score 88 runs in total. At the close of play on day two, Northants had scored 40 runs and had lost 7 wickets. Gloucestershire must have been hopeful of gaining a famous victory, but, unfortunately, rain meant there was no play on the final day, and the match was drawn. (www.cricketarchive.com)

JUNE 12TH

1856: The Dean and Chapter of Gloucester sent a petition to the Queen, calling for their diocese to be separated from Bristol. One Bishop had held both sees since 1836, when James Henry Monk was consecrated Bishop of Gloucester and Bristol. Monk died on June 6th 1856, and Gloucester resolved to plead its case before the next Bishop was chosen. It was argued that the Bishop had rarely visited Gloucester, preferring Bristol; that both sees could support separate Bishops if their estates were properly managed; and that the Church of England as a whole would benefit from smaller bishoprics. The petition was unsuccessful and the two bishoprics were not separated until 1897, when Bishop Ellicott resigned the see of Bristol. (*Fasti Ecclesiae Anglicanae, 1541-1837*, Volume 8, ed. J.M. Horn, 1996)

JUNE 13TH

1879: The following advertisements appeared in the 'Wanted' columns of *The Citizen*:

- Wanted, by respectable Married Man, middle-aged situation to look after Horse or Cow, no objection to make himself generally useful.
- Wanted, Furnished Apartments, near Railway Station; the applicant will want breakfast, tea and supper only; from home about three days per week.
- Wanted, to purchase, a good yellow Hen Canary, 12 months old.
- Wanted immediately, for the Sea Side, a useful Maid, strong and healthy, very dark complexion, height five feet seven inches, with good references.
- Wanted, a respectable, healthy, willing, good-tempered person, to undertake the household duties of a small family, work light, moderate salary.
- Wanted, by a Young Lady, aged nineteen, a situation in a Confectioners or Fancy Shop, not been out before; could give a little time, in the neighbourhood of Cheltenham or Gloucester preferred; indoors; good references.

JUNE 14TH

1713: Sir John Powell, judge, died. He was born in 1645 in Gloucester, where his father was an alderman and once served as Mayor. He trained as a lawyer, becoming a member of the Inner Temple, and was called to the bar in 1671. In 1674, he was elected as Town Clerk of Gloucester. From June 1702, Powell became a judge in the Court of Common Pleas, and of the Queen's Bench.

In the courts, Powell gained a reputation for being fair and humane. When a woman on a charge of witchcraft was alleged to be able to fly, the judge said, 'You may – there is no law against flying'. Author Jonathan Swift, who met Powell in his later years, described him as 'an old fellow with grey hairs, who was the merriest old gentleman I ever saw, spoke pleasing things, and chuckled till he cried.'

Judge Powell died at his house in Gloucester. A monument to him was put up in the Cathedral. (*Oxford Dictionary of National Biography*)

JUNE 15TH

1904: At the Gloucester Petty Sessions, James Egerton, a hawker of Westgate Street, was summonsed under the Fishery Act, for selling elvers in the close season. Benjamin Keates, water bailiff, prosecuted for the Severn Fishery Board. Inspector Dennis said he saw the defendant selling elvers in the street on April 28th, which was the first day of the close season, and told him he was doing wrong. The defendant said he didn't know he was breaking the law, and asked if he might sell what he had in the cart, on condition he sold no more. The Inspector gave him permission to sell what he had, but a few days later, he saw more elvers for sale outside the defendant's shop.

Egerton said that for twenty-five years he had never been stopped selling elvers at that time of year before. He said he was very sorry, but he had always understood he could take elvers until he received notice from the Board. He was fined 5 shillings, plus 7 shillings costs. (*The Citizen*)

JUNE 16TH

1806: A dentist named Jones advertised that he could be seen at Brown's Ironmongers in Eastgate Street. Among his services, he could scale and clean teeth, transplant natural teeth, set artificial teeth to the greatest nicety, and fill hollow teeth with gold, silver or lead. Mr Jones requested that those ladies and gentlemen who might wish to honour him with a visit, should not delay too long, as his stay in town would be short. (*Gloucester Journal*)

———— •◆• ————

1893: At the Northgate Wesleyan Chapel, the Revd Peter Mackenzie, a popular preacher and speaker, gave a lecture. Mr Mackenzie was already known by reputation to the people of Gloucester, and there was a large congregation in attendance. The programme was started with a short service, followed by a sermon by Mr Mackenzie. Then the special guest gave his lecture, on Jeroboam and the worshipping of idols.

The Citizen commented that the way in which the popular preacher dealt with scripture history was unique and fascinating. Mr Mackenzie was gifted with a truly marvellous flow of language, and his comments gave rise to frequent applause and irresistible laughter. (*The Citizen*)

JUNE 17TH

1889: Eugenio Marchetti, an Italian ice-cream seller, aged 15, appeared at Gloucester Magistrates' Court, charged with assaulting Felice Fazzi, another Italian ice-cream seller, by shooting a revolver at him on the previous Saturday. Fazzi was the boy's employer until Marchetti left him and set up his own business. While Fazzi was serving customers in the street, the prisoner had fired three shots at him; Fazzi protected himself by holding up the back of his cart. The prisoner fired another shot, which hit the head of Fazzi's pony. He fired two more shots at the victim, one of which grazed his thigh. The prisoner was remanded in custody to be tried at the next assizes.

In July, Marchetti appeared at the Gloucester Assizes, charged with shooting at Fazzi with intent to do him grievous bodily harm. The prisoner pleaded guilty to a second, lesser charge of common assault. The court heard that there had been various quarrels between the two. Marchetti said he had only meant to frighten Fazzi. He was found not guilty of intent to cause grievous bodily harm and was sentenced to one month's hard labour for committing an assault. The judge commented that it was unfortunate that weapons like these could be obtained so easily in the city. (*Bristol Mercury*)

JUNE 18TH

1927: A letter in *The Citizen*, written by 'RATEPAYER', of Dean's Way, Gloucester, commented on the example of modern town planning, which could be seen in the area of Dean's Walk and Dean's Way, where some new residences were being built. The writer wondered what the people who supported open spaces, rather than the crowded slum areas built many years ago, thought of the houses now under construction, especially those in Dean's Way. Some of the houses would not have sufficient garden to swing a cat in, much less to hang out washing to dry.

The writer thought it would have been better to link up Dean's Walk with Dean's Way by building the same style of houses as those already existing, keeping them all uniform, and at the same time allow the tenants to have fair-sized gardens. The houses appeared to have been planned in a very haphazard manner, devoid of uniformity or system, the one desire being to crowd as many houses into as small a space as possible. The Corporation's intention was to abolish slums forever, not to clear one and establish others a few years later. Ratepayers should 'complain about the way that those who are supposed to be in authority are making districts look so hideous'. (*The Citizen*)

JUNE 19TH

1891: The City Coroner held three inquests in the evening. The first two took place at the Ship Inn, the Quay, starting with the death of an 8-year-old boy, Joseph Henry Best, who had been seen to fall into the water while playing in the Great West yard at the Docks. His body was found four days later. The jury returned a verdict of 'accidently drowned'.

The second inquest was on Henry White of Arlingham, who was 23 and worked on the trow, Exeter. His body had been recovered from the docks that morning. White had been drinking at the East End Vaults in Barton Street on the night he disappeared. A verdict of 'found dead' was returned, as there was no evidence as to how he got into the water.

The third inquest was held at the Crown and Thistle Inn in Barton Street, on Alfred Elliott, who had died there suddenly on June 16th. Aged 28 and a lamplighter, he was generally fit and healthy, although he had complained of a pain in his stomach on the day he died. He went to the inn with a friend, where he collapsed and died. The coroner said there was no doubt that death was caused by heart disease, accelerated by Elliott's constant movements as a lamplighter. A verdict was reached of 'died suddenly of natural causes'. (*The Citizen*)

JUNE 20TH

1736: George Whitefield was ordained as a deacon by the Bishop of Gloucester, Martin Benson, in the Cathedral. Born on December 16th 1714 at the Bell Inn in Southgate Street, he was the sixth child of Thomas and Elizabeth Whitefield. His father was innkeeper at the Bell Inn and a wine merchant. He attended the Crypt School, and then in 1732, aged 17, went to Pembroke College, Oxford, as a servitor (meaning he received free tuition in return for waiting on wealthier students), where he met John and Charles Wesley, the founders of Methodism.

The week after being ordained, he preached his first sermon at St Mary de Crypt Church, where he had been baptised. His powers as an orator had an enormous impact on his audience. Later, he came to prefer outdoor preaching, like his friends the Wesleys, and spoke to large crowds in the Gloucester area in the late 1730s and early 1740s. He gained a reputation as an astounding preacher, attracting audiences of 20,000 in London. He went on to preach in America. Although Whitefield was a minister of the Church of England, with the Wesleys he helped inspire the movement which became Methodism. He formed, and was president of, the first Methodist conference. He died in 1770. (*Oxford Dictionary of National Biography*)

JUNE 21ST

1865: Albert Herbert Brewer was born in Gloucester. As a boy, he attended the King's School, and was a chorister at the Cathedral, where he studied under the organist C.H. Lloyd. He acted as organist at St Catherine's and St Mary de Crypt churches when he was 15. He received the first ever organist scholarship to the Royal College of Music. Before becoming the organist at Gloucester Cathedral in 1896, he held the post at Bristol Cathedral, at St Michael's, Coventry, and at Tonbridge School.

In Gloucester, Brewer became an important influence on musical activity in the city. As the Cathedral organist, he took on the customary role of conductor of the Three Choirs Festival, in the years when the event took place in Gloucester. He also founded the Gloucester Orpheus Society and the Gloucestershire Orchestral Society. His compositions included the oratario *Emmaus*, which was orchestrated by Elgar. He was knighted in 1926, and died in Gloucester, on March 1st 1928. (*Oxford Dictionary of National Biography*)

JUNE 22ND

1893: The Second Volunteer Battalion, Gloucestershire Regiment, held its third annual prize-meeting at the Over Range. A large number of competitors from Cheltenham, Tewkesbury and Stroud, as well as from Gloucester, took part. The weather was not ideal for shooting, as there was a changeable wind and variable light. Top place in the shooting match went to Private C.F. Green, who scored 93 points, and won £4.

After the shooting, the annual meeting was held. The Honorary Secretary, the above-mentioned Private Green, presented the balance sheet and report, and said that after the year's expenses had been paid, there would be a balance of about £8 to carry forward to the next season. The report showed that the shooting of the battalion for the last season was of a very high standard, as it had succeeded in winning the Ranelagh Challenge Plate at Bisley. It was proposed, and unanimously agreed, that old Volunteers who had served in the regiment for fifteen years should be allowed to join the association as 'veterans', and enjoy all the privileges of the same. (*The Citizen*)

JUNE 23RD

1909: King Edward VII visited the Royal Agricultural Show, which was held at Gloucester. He travelled to the city by train, arriving at the Great Western Railway station. He attended civic receptions at the Guildhall and Shire Hall, before driving in his Windsor landau, escorted by the Royal Gloucestershire Hussars, through the highly decorated streets of the city, cheered by crowds of people who had lined the streets to see him. Arriving at the showground at Oxlease, he was met by Sir Gilbert Grenell and conducted to the Royal Pavillion, where the Duke of Devonshire and other members of the Council of the Royal Society received him. (*Cheltenham Looker-on*)

———◆———

2002: A bronze statue of the Roman Emperor Nerva on his horse was lowered into place on a concrete plinth in Southgate Street. Nerva had given Gloucester (*Glevum*) the status of a Colonia in AD 96. A Colonia was a high-status city, providing a place of settlement for retired elite soldiers, and its inhabitants enjoyed the full rights of Roman citizenship.

The statue had been commissioned by the Gloucester Civic Trust, and the sculptor was Anthony Stone. Underneath the statue, a time capsule was placed, containing books, newspapers, poetry, and other items, including a Gloucester rugby shirt and a pair of Marks & Spencer underpants. (www.visit-gloucestershire.co.uk)

JUNE 24TH

1783: Following several visits to Gloucester County Gaol in the Castle by the prison reformer, John Howard, new rules were brought in for the Keeper of the Gaol, which came into effect on this day. Previously, the gaoler had received no salary, except for £10 a year for keeping the bridewell. Instead, he could charge prisoners fees, and he had a licence to sell beer in the prison. When Howard visited in December 1782, he found some improvements had been made, but a number of townspeople were drinking in the gaol taproom. The new rules stated that the gaol keeper was to receive an annual salary of £60 a year, but he could no longer charge prisoners fees, sell liquor, or permit gambling in the gaol. (Whiting, J.R.S., *Prison Reform in Gloucestershire, 1776-1829*, 1975)

JUNE 25TH

1846: Gloucester was visited by one of the most violent storms of thunder and lightening ever remembered. It had been a fine morning, but towards noon, threatening clouds began to gather, and shortly after there was a vivid flash of lightening, followed immediately by a tremendous clap of thunder. This was succeeded by three or four others, which shook nearly every house in the city. There was also a violent hailstorm, which lasted about fifteen minutes.

At the Spa turnpike gate, on the new Stroud Road, electricity from the lightening hit the roof of the house. It descended through the bedroom into the kitchen, where there were about a dozen people, most of whom had gone in there to shelter from the storm. Everyone, except for an infant about two weeks old, was injured, but no one was killed. The greater part of the front wall was blown out and all the windows were shattered. Luckily, the house had only been erected a few years before and was substantially built, otherwise the whole building could have been completely destroyed. Medical aid arrived quickly and seven people were taken to the Infirmary. Three of them were discharged the same evening, and those who were kept in all recovered.

It was reported that another person was struck by lightening at Barnwood. His clothes were burnt, but he wasn't injured. (*Bristol Mercury*)

JUNE 26TH

1906: The Gloucester City and Swimming Club held a display at the Public Baths, at which they had a very special guest, in the person of J.A. Jarvis, an ex-amateur Champion of the World and regarded as the greatest swimmer of his generation. The very large audience which attended was treated to an excellent display by the champion and his 8-year-old daughter.

The Citizen believed that it would have done the club a great deal of good to have had a man of Jarvis's standing perform. It would persuade parents to make sure that their children learnt to swim, and was a strong recommendation for learning life-saving skills. Jarvis's daughter had demonstrated in the display that she could 'save' a full-grown man if necessary.

Other events of the evening included the Club Handicap, raced between the club members, a team race between Southgate and Sir Thomas Rich's, won by the former, and a quarter-mile invitation scratch race. The programme concluded with a water-polo match between Gloucester and Bristol, which the home team won. (*The Citizen*)

JUNE 27TH

1899: Two circus acts came to Gloucester, one being Barnum and Bailey's 'Greatest Show on Earth' and the other Lord George Sanger's Circus. Barnum and Bailey's circus had visited Gloucester eight months earlier, and did not attract a capacity crowd on this occasion. Sanger, who called himself 'the world's greatest showman', arrived in Gloucester with his circus at 7 o'clock in the morning, having travelled from Ross-on-Wye.

Lord Sanger said it had been fifty-five years to the day since his first appearance in Gloucester with a circus. Referring to the rival attraction, he said he would go fifty miles out of his way to perform in a town on the same day as 'the greatest show on earth'. Indeed, he was supposed to have been performing at Ross today, but had come to Gloucester early, because he couldn't forgo the pleasure of meeting his old friend, Mr Bailey.

The greatest attraction of Sanger's Circus was the grand naval and military spectacle, *With Kitchener to Khartoum*, featuring a fleet of gunboats, as well as 700 men and women, horses, elephants and camels. After the show at Gloucester, Sanger's moved on to Cheltenham – as did Barnum and Bailey's. (*The Citizen*)

JUNE 28TH

1880: Celebrations were held nationally in this year, to mark the centenary of the Sunday School movement. In Gloucester on this day, Lord Shaftesbury unveiled a model of a statue of Robert Raikes. It was intended that it would be placed in the Cathedral, but this never happened. A statue was put up on Victoria Embankment in London, however, and in 1930, a replica of this was placed in the Park. The centenary celebrations continued through the week, with a grand service at the Cathedral on the next day, a conference at Shire Hall on June 30th, and a children's service at the Cathedral on July 1st. (*The Graphic*)

———•◆•———

1864: The funeral took place of the Reverend Canon Calderbank, Roman Catholic priest at Gloucester, who had died suddenly. He was buried at the cemetery. Previous to the interment, a requiem mass was celebrated at St Peter's Roman Catholic Church, by the Hon. and Revd W. Clifford, Bishop of Clifton, assisted by almost twenty priests from Hereford and the surrounding district. A great number of the shops were partially closed as a mark of respect. (*The Citizen*)

JUNE 29TH

1849: John Phillpotts, Member of Parliament for Gloucester City from 1830 to 1847, died suddenly on an omnibus in London, aged 74. He was the son of another John Phillpotts, who came to Gloucester in the 1780s and ran the Bell Inn. John junior trained as a barrister, while his brother entered the Church and eventually became the Bishop of Exeter. At the time of his election in 1830, John Phillpotts was said to have spent a great deal of money on bribes. The *Birmingham Journal* reported that thirty freemen canvassing on his behalf had spent £310 in ten days on refreshments, and one of them had died of excess as a result. (*The Citizen*; *Birmingham Journal*)

1882: A letter was published in *The Citizen*, written by the vicar of St Luke's, concerning rumours of the prevalence of scarlet fever in New Street. He said there had been nine deaths in the street, all children under 8 years old. Three of them had come from one house, which was overcrowded and had defective drainage. St Luke's schools were closing that day for the summer holidays, which was the day originally planned, and would re-open in three weeks.

Scarlet fever had been around in the Gloucester area since September 1881, and there had been twenty-two deaths by the end of that year. By the end of 1882, there had been another forty-two deaths. (*The Citizen*)

JUNE 30TH

1949: The Duke of Beaufort unveiled the new plaques which had been put onto the War Memorial, listing the names of those who had died in the Second World War. Hundreds of people gathered to witness the ceremony, including an invited party of 350 relatives and friends of those whose names were on the plaques, which were placed below those for the First World War. One small boy was wearing his father's medals. Also there were units of armed forces, pre-service and ex-service organisations, and ministers of the Church of England and of other denominations.

The Duke, with the Mayor and Corporation, walked in procession from the Guildhall to the Memorial, where they were met by the Duchess of Beaufort, the Mayoress and other ladies. After the plaques had been unveiled, the Mayor laid a wreath, then many of the relatives laid floral tributes to their loved ones, watched in silence by the official party. (*Gloucester Journal*)

———◆———

1874: On the first day of the Gloucestershire Quarter Sessions, a discussion took place regarding a report on the county prisons, in which it was stated that the use of Australian mutton had meant a saving of £50 during the past year. The health of the prisoners had been well maintained under this dietary regime, and it was agreed to apply to the Home Secretary to sanction its continued use. (*The Citizen*)

JULY 1ST

1903: Buffalo Bill's Wild West Show came to Gloucester. An advertisement announced that the show, consisting of four special trains, 500 horses, and 800 people, including 100 American Indians, was visiting only principal cities and greater railway centres. As well as exhibitions of the riding skills of the various participants, the show carried out enactments of scenes of border life, including a stagecoach hold-up, riding bucking broncos, and attacks on emigrant trains. The vast arena was illuminated at night by two special electric light plants.

On the morning of the show, the company arrived at Gloucester by train in the early hours, having played in Cheltenham the night before. During the morning, Gloucester folk were treated to the sight of participants in the show travelling to the ground at Kingsholm on horseback, including North American Indians, Cossacks, Bedouins and cowboys.

In both the afternoon and evening performances, Colonel Cody (aka Buffalo Bill) made appearances, introducing his 'rough riders' of many nationalities, and doing some shooting with his favourite Winchester. Before the vast audience had cleared the ground, vehicles, horses and performers were making their way to the railway station, to travel to their next show, in Hereford. (*The Citizen*)

July 2nd

1887: The final day of a county cricket match between Gloucestershire and Yorkshire took place at the Spa ground. Before lunch, there had been a slight chance that the visitors might win, but W.G. Grace placed the issue beyond doubt. In the first innings, Grace had scored 92 runs. In the second innings, after being in for three hours and forty minutes, he passed his century. Griffiths was the last man in, and Grace marked his arrival by hitting a ball into the press tent. It looked like W.G. would reach a second century, but when he was on 183, Griffiths was caught, giving the home side a total score of 338. Grace was loudly cheered for his play. He had gone in to bat when one wicket was down, and had carried his bat right through the innings without giving a chance. He had also taken a wicket during the Yorkshire innings. The match was called a draw. (*The Citizen*)

JULY 3RD

1885: Charles Povey appeared at the City Petty Sessions, charged with being helplessly drunk in the public streets on the previous night. The defendant said that 'he'd had a drop that came over him'. PC McCarthey said he found the defendant lying on the ground in a helpless drunken condition in St Catherine Street. Povey said he had left the workhouse that morning to find work. He was fined *2s 6d* plus costs, or seven days' imprisonment.

Also before the magistrates was William Organ, of Llanthony, who was summonsed for being quarrelsome and refusing to quit the Wheatsheaf Inn at Littleworth on June 15th. He pleaded guilty. The defendant and another man had been involved in the incident. The other man had been summonsed soon after the event, but the defendant had been away at Sharpness. The landlord of the Wheatsheaf Inn gave evidence in support of the summons, but did not press the case. Organ received the same sentence as Povey. (*The Citizen*)

July 4th

1871: Hubert Cecil Booth was born in Theresa Place, Gloucester, the son of Abraham Booth, a timber importer. The family moved to Belle Vue House in Spa Road, and later to No. 27 St Michael's Square. Booth studied for a City and Guilds qualification in London and became a mechanical and civil engineer. In 1901, he patented his design for a motorised vacuum cleaner. He came up with the idea after seeing a demonstration of a cleaner in London. The device attempted to blow dust into a container, but most of it went over the spectators. Booth thought a suction system would be more effective. His patent for a cleaning machine consisted of a large, horse-drawn, petrol-driven unit, which was parked outside the building to be cleaned, then long hoses were fed through the windows. The first horse-drawn, petrol-driven model, nicknamed 'the Puffing Billy', was replaced in 1904 by an electric-powered domestic model, and in 1921 by an upright version. Booth coined the term 'vacuum cleaner' when he formed The Vacuum Cleaner Company Ltd after patenting his device. (*Oxford Dictionary of National Biography*; www. thecityofgloucester.co.uk)

July 5th

1828: On this night, several men were employed in clearing a soil-pit on the Quay, and had removed the contents to within a foot of the bottom. One of them, John Steele, descended into the vault to complete the work, and was rendered senseless by the effects of the foul air. A fellow labourer, David Watkins, went to his assistance and shared the same fate. A third man, Samuel Powick, went down to try to help his workmates, and he also was overcome. A fourth worker, Edward Cornwall, let down a ladder, and he managed to bring Powick up. He was taken home and seen by a doctor, but died within two hours. Steele and Watkins were dead before they were brought out of the vault, which was not more than 8 feet deep. (*Gloucester Journal*)

1919: A tank, stripped of its engine, was given by the National War Savings Committee to the Gloucester War Savings Association, as a permanent war memorial for the city. It was received by the Mayor and Corporation and placed in the Public Park. It stood near the Wellington Street entrance until the Second World War, when it was scrapped to make weapons. (*Western Daily Press*; Voyce, J., *The City of Gloucester*, 1995)

JULY 6TH

1887: The Western Counties and South Wales Telephone Company opened a new trunk line from Bristol to Gloucester. The company had joined various towns by trunk lines since 1885. The first had run from Bristol to Sharpness, then an extension had been put in, which ran over the Severn to Lydney and Wales; now another extension had been added at Sharpness, which went to Gloucester. There were already twenty subscribers to the new line. Mr Henry Fedden and Mr Pole were at the Bristol head offices, while at the Gloucester office in Berkeley Street were Mr H.F. Lewis, manager of the telephone company, Mr Vasser-Smith, Mayor of Gloucester, and a number of residents. The Bristol office then received a call from the Gloucester Mayor, expressing the thanks of the people of Gloucester for this bond of communication between the two cities. Mr Lewis later spoke through the telephone to the members of the press in Bristol. (*Bristol Mercury*)

———— • ◆ • ————

1844: The Bristol and Gloucester Railway opened on this day. Six trains a day ran between the two cities, and the stations along the line were Yate, Wickwar, Charfield, Dursley, Berkeley, Frocester and Stonehouse. (*Gloucester Journal*)

July 7th

1892: This was the opening day of an exhibition of gas cooking and heating stoves, domestic appliances, and food and cookery, which ran at Gloucester Corn Exchange until July 12th. Miss Maud Lewis, of the Nottingham School of Cookery, lectured on cookery in the afternoons and evenings, and the Eureka gas cooker, on hire from the Gloucester Gas Company, was shown in action and explained. Free tasting sessions were a major attraction at the event. Admission was free, although there was a small charge for people using the front seats. (*The Citizen*)

1900: The annual Church Parade of the Gloucester Friendly and Trade Societies took place on this Sunday. The event created a great deal of interest in the city. About 400 Brethren, representing twenty-five societies, met in the Spa field at 2 o'clock, and formed themselves into a procession which made its way to the Cathedral, headed by the Civic military band and the All Saints' drum and fife band. The procession stopped at the Guildhall, where it was joined by the Mayor, the City High Sheriff, and members of the Corporation.

The service at the Cathedral was of 'a most hearty character'. After leaving the Cathedral, the procession went via Westgate Street, Eastgate Street and Barton Street, to the Spa Pump Room, where they dispersed. (*The Citizen*)

JULY 8TH

1836: The *Gloucester Journal* reported on an inquest held at the county gaol on a prisoner who had died while waiting for his trial. David James, aged 29, had been charged with committing bigamy, by marrying Ann Mercer on May 9th, when his former wife was still alive. The inquest decided that James's death was occasioned by 'an affection of the brain, produced by nervous excitement, on account of his imprisonment'. (*Gloucester Journal*)

———◆———

1872: Gloucester Theatre Royal put on a rare treat for its visitors, in the form of a performance by Mr J.L. Toole, supported by members of the Gaiety company. The pieces presented were *The Weavers*, scenes from *Paul Pry*, the trial scene from *Pickwick Papers* and *That Blessed Baby*. Mr Toole was in his happiest mood, and convulsed the audience with his broad humour. Each of his portrayals was greeted with loud applause and recalls. The house was, a reporter said, 'crammed to suffocation'.

Miss Tremaine, a member of the Gaiety company, created a very favourable impression both through her acting and her singing. She was encored after performing *Cherry Ripe*, and then sang *Within a Mile of Edinburgh Town*, which she was also asked to repeat. The unanimous opinion was that Miss Tremaine had a bright future before her. (*The Era*)

JULY 9TH

1946: At the City Magistrates' Court, the Chairman, Mr Tom Bell, commented that the problem of car parking in Gloucester was becoming acute, with the increasing number of vehicles on the road. His remarks were a response to a number of people who had appeared before him on that day, charged with parking offences.

The defendants had all been summonsed for parking their vehicles on the side of Clarence Street, on which parking was not allowed on the particular day in question. The prosecutions were the first that had been made in connection with this matter, although the order regulating parking in Clarence Street had been in operation for three years. During that time, the police had issued a considerable number of written cautions, but this hadn't achieved the desired effect. (*Gloucester Journal*)

July 10th

1832: Ann Yarnold, from Worcester, was arrested in Gloucester for robbing a farmer of cash at a fair. She had enticed the man into a passageway, where she had contrived to abstract the money from his pockets. Yarnold was an old offender in this type of robbery, and for some time past had been making a circuit of the fairs, races, and other public occasions in the neighbouring cities and towns. She had recently spent a year in Hereford gaol for attempting to rob an excise officer in that city. (*Gloucester Journal*)

———— ◆ ————

1903: The death was recorded at Gloucester Workhouse of George Shergold, aged 75, who had succumbed to heart disease. Until about a year previously, he had lived at New Street, Gloucester. He was a shoemaker by trade, but was best known in Gloucester for being the inventor of 'Shergold's Original Safety Bicycle'. This machine possessed all the essential points of modern safety, including front steering, rear and chain driving, and geared up and rotary action. (*The Citizen*)

JULY 11TH

1853: The show organised by the South Wales and West Midlands Branch of the Royal Agricultural Society opened in Gloucester. The site at Bristol Road was impressive, covering about 17 acres, with a main avenue, 30 feet wide, running the whole length of the ground.

The first day was occupied with trials of agricultural implements and machines, and the whole of the trial grounds and yards were scenes of great activity. In addition to the trial areas in the showground, three pieces of arable land close by were also used, one for trials of implements for heavy soils, another for clod-crushers, rollers, etc., and the third for tools for light soil. A competition between four ploughs was very close, and great interest was shown in Mr Richardson's new digging machine, which was intended to supersede the work of the plough. About a dozen reaping machines were put to work in a field of barley, witnessed by numerous spectators, many of whom believed that such inventions would never be able to do the work as well as it was done by hand. (*Bath Chronicle*)

July 12th

1892: The new Gloucester Municipal Building, to be known as The Guildhall, was officially opened, after two years of building work on the site of the old Sir Thomas Rich's School in Eastgate Street. Those who had previously only seen the narrow frontage of the building were surprised at how extensive and spacious it was inside, with its depth running from Eastgate Street to New Inn Lane. The ground floor was allocated to corporation offices, while the council chamber, committee rooms, Mayor's parlour and the public hall were on the first floor. On a floor above were additional offices, caretaker's quarters and kitchens. Each floor was provided with retiring rooms and lavatories.

An inaugural banquet was held that evening in the banqueting hall, attended by more than 200 guests of the Mayor. Toasts were made to the Queen, the Prince and Princess of Wales and the rest of the Royal Family, the Lord Bishop, Clergy and ministers, and the Army, Navy and Reserve Forces.

The Guildhall was the main office for the city council until 1986, when it moved into Herbert Warehouse at Gloucester Docks. (*The Citizen*; *A History of the County of Gloucester, Volume IV, The City of Gloucester*, ed. N.M. Herbert, 1988)

JULY 13TH

1381: Thomas Woodstock, the Earl of Buckingham, stayed overnight at Llanthony Priory. He had assumed patronage of the priory through his marriage to Eleanor, daughter of Humphrey Bohun, the former patron. The prior at that time, William Chirton, was anxious to have the goodwill of the Earl, who was the uncle of King Richard II. Woodstock arrived at Llanthony with 200 soldiers, having travelled from Essex, where his army had killed 500 supporters of the Peasant's Revolt.

On the next day, the Earl and his wife, and his knights and their squires and pages, were admitted into the priory's spiritual fraternity, which meant they could participate in all masses, prayers, fasts, etc., performed by the brethren, and have prayers said for them. On July 15th, Woodstock held an inquiry at Gloucester, attended by the whole town, with the purpose of detecting rebels. This resulted in five burgesses being arrested on charges of sedition. They were tried at Llanthony and sentenced to imprisonment in Gloucester Castle. ('The Pleas of St Kyneburgh: Gloucester v Llanthony Priory, 1390-2', by John Rhodes, in *Archives & Local History in Bristol & Gloucestershire*, ed. J. Bettey, Bristol and Gloucestershire Archaeological Society, 2007)

July 14th

1925: A memorial stone was laid by councillors at the site of the new Kingsholm School, in Worcester Street. An elementary school had been planned for the Kingsholm area since 1908, and the site was bought in 1914. The school was eventually opened on October 11th 1926, by the Mayor, William Jones. He opened the main door of the building with a presentation key, handed to him by the architect.

The school began as a mixed infants' school, but in 1931 it became a senior girls' and infants' school. In 1939, the boys from Archdeacon Street School were moved to Kingsholm, and it became senior mixed and infants. Under the 1944 Education Act, Kingsholm became a mixed secondary modern, but in 1957, the girls were relocated to Barnwood. It remained as a boys' secondary school until it closed in 1973.

In 1979, the building became the County Record Office, now called Gloucestershire Archives. (*Western Daily Press*; *A History of the County of Gloucester, Volume IV: The City of Gloucester*, ed. N.M. Herbert, 1988)

JULY 15TH

1100: The Abbey of St Peter (later Gloucester Cathedral) was consecrated by the Bishop of Worcester, assisted by the Bishops of Rochester, Hereford and Bangor. Eight hundred years later, on Sunday, July 15th 1900, special consecration anniversary services were held at the Cathedral in the morning, afternoon and evening. (*The Citizen*)

———◆———

1739: John Wesley preached in Gloucester for the first time. He and his brother Charles were friends of Gloucester-born George Whitefield, who introduced them to the city. John Wesley made infrequent visits for the next twenty-five years, only preaching at Gloucester again in 1744 and 1766. After 1777, support for Wesleyan Methodism in the city grew and Wesley preached there regularly from then. (*A History of the County of Gloucester, Volume IV, The City of Gloucester*, ed. N.M. Herbert, 1988)

———◆———

1832: The burial registers of St Mary de Crypt Church in Southgate Street recorded the interment of Isabella White, aged 31. She was not buried in the churchyard, however, but at the Infirmary ground, and a letter 'C' marked in the margin indicated that she had died of cholera. A total of fourteen cholera victims were recorded in the register between July 15th and September 1st, of whom five were buried in the Infirmary ground, and the rest at Longford. (Gloucestershire Archives, Parish Registers, P151/11 IN 1/13)

JULY 16TH

1798: A notice in the *Gloucester Journal* informed readers that the famous actress, Mrs Siddons, was to appear at the Theatre Royal, for two nights only, her first performance being on Wednesday, July 18th. She was to play the part of Calista in *The Fair Repentent*. Mrs Siddons alternated her performances in Gloucester with dates in Cheltenham, where she appeared on three nights in the same role. (*Gloucester Journal*)

———◆———

1889: A large proportion of the population of Hucclecote left their village to go on a day-trip. The chief organisers of the excursion were the vicar, Revd Heath, and Messrs F. Hannam-Clarke, Conway Jones and Corbett. Their destination was to be Sharpness Point.

At Gloucester, the party went down the canal on the steamboat *Wave*, which had been prettily decorated by Messrs Conway Jones and Co., accompanied by the band of the Gloucester Artillery. The boat left Gloucester at 8 o'clock and arrived at Sharpness about two hours and thirty minutes later. The Docks entrance, pier, and shipping were all viewed with great interest. In the afternoon, they went to Berkeley Castle and looked round the town, and in the evening they sat down to tea at Sharpness pleasure grounds. They returned on the *Wave* and the *Lapwing*.

The total number who went on the trip was approximately 250, and the population of Hucclecote was only about 386. (*The Citizen*)

July 17th

1831: A storm hit Gloucester, with Quedgeley being the most greatly effected area. The terrible weather came in from the east in the afternoon, with heavy thunder and vivid lightening, but the worst element was hail, which fell for nearly an hour, causing enormous destruction. Many hailstones were over 3 inches in circumference, and caused extensive damage to the growing crops. Wheat and beans in many instances were completely severed. In gardens, also, a great deal of damage was done. Over 200 panes of glass were broken in the greenhouse of Mrs Curtis Hayward. (*Gloucester Journal*)

———— • ◆ • ————

1899: At the Petty Sessions, John and Charlotte McDermot, of no fixed address, were charged with assaulting William Jones, a verger at Gloucester Cathedral. On the night in question, Mr Jones was informed that two people were lying in Palace Yard, full-stretch across the pavement, with the man's head being in the woman's lap. When he asked them to leave, the man rushed at him and tried to get his head between the verger's legs to throw him. As Jones defended himself, the woman scratched his face and sank her teeth into his arm. In court, the woman said the verger had hit her on the head with a stick, but he said he had merely tapped her head with his cane when she was biting him. The defendants were fined 5 shillings each. (*The Citizen*)

JULY 18TH

1761: Gloucester Infirmary opened on this day. In 1752, Bishop Martin Benson had bequeathed in his will £200 towards founding an infirmary. A temporary infirmary was opened at the Crown and Sceptre Inn, in Lower Westgate Street, and a committee was formed to raise further funds to construct a purpose-built hospital. The infirmary was intended to be for patients who were unable to pay for medical treatment. Entry was by ticket, given out by subscribers to the institution.

In 1756, the governors acquired a lease for a site in Southgate Street, and King George II gave timber from the Forest of Dean for the building work. Patients were admitted from 1761, and the temporary infirmary was closed. From 1948, the Infirmary amalgamated with Gloucester City General Hospital, and from 1949 was known as Gloucestershire Royal Hospital. The wards in Southgate Street finally closed in 1975. (*A History of the County of Gloucester, Volume IV: The City of Gloucester*, ed. N.M. Herbert, 1988)

JULY 19TH

1900: The Gloucester Electricity Works in Commercial Road were formally opened in the afternoon. This was a civic occasion, because the Gloucester Corporation had decided to control its own electricity supply, rather than allowing a private company to do so. In the evening, a banquet was held at the Guildhall, hosted by the Chairman of the Electricity Supply Company, Councillor Clutterbuck. Also in attendance were the Consulting Engineer (Robert Hammonds), the architect (Harry A. Dancey), and all of the contractors

At the top table were Mr Clutterbuck, the Mayor of Gloucester, the City High Sheriff, the Mayors of Cheltenham, Mansfield and Worcester, and various members of the Church, aldermen and councillors. Many toasts were made, including one proposed by the Mayor, of 'Success to the Electricity Undertaking'. He said he would like to take an early opportunity in congratulating the citizens upon having an electric light station established in their midst. (*The Citizen*)

JULY 20TH

2007: Torrential rain all day caused flooding throughout Gloucestershire, with Gloucester itself being very badly affected. By the afternoon of the first day, which was a Friday, floodwater was waist-deep in parts of the city, and more than 400 homes had to be evacuated. By the following Monday, there were fears that Gloucester's water supply was set to run dry, as the Mythe pumping station near Tewkesbury was flooded and put out of action. Water tanks were brought in and bottled water was distributed.

On July 23rd, military and emergency staff were fighting to save a major electricity sub-station in Gloucester from flooding. The Prime Minister, Gordon Brown, visited, joining the scores of press reporters who were already in the city. By July 25th, bowsers were in place in many of the city's street and suburbs, although complaints were growing that the tanks were not being topped up often enough. At this point, 140,000 homes were without water. The next day, the Prime Minister visited again, as did members of the Royal Family. Finally, the Mythe pumping station was put back into action and the water supply was turned back on in Gloucester's houses and businesses. (*The Citizen*)

JULY 21ST

1866: At the County Petty Sessions, two men named Townsend and Limbrick were committed for trial at the Quarter Sessions. They had been in the habit of stripping and running races on the turnpike roads, wearing only loincloths made of gauze. This 'filthy conduct' had annoyed dozens of respectable people, and it was hoped that they would be well punished.

The two men had to wait in gaol for nearly three months before the next court of Quarter Sessions was held at Gloucester, and then the Grand Jury decided that their case should not go to trial. (*Western Daily Press*)

1892: The Gloucester and District Perfect Thrift Building Society held a public ballot in the Barton Hall. Councillor John Allen, Chairman of the Directors, presided, supported by the Vice-Chairman and other directors. There was a fairly large attendance. The Chairman, Vice-Chairman and director Mr Williams addressed the meeting and explained the principles and working of the society.

During the evening, the ballot took place, and share number 606 was drawn, the winner being James Myerscough, of Clement Street, Gloucester. He had only been a member for a short time, but was now entitled to an interest-free loan of £100, repayable in six years and eight months. The Chairman announced that another ballot would take place at the same place in about six weeks' time. (*The Citizen*)

JULY 22ND

1796: On this day, a prisoner named Kidd Wake was made to stand in the pillory in Eastgate Street, as part of his sentence. Wake was a state prisoner who had committed his crime in London. He had been arrested after an incident on October 19th 1795, when he was among a crowd who hooted and jeered at King George III, shouting 'No war!', as he went to and from Parliament. Stones were thrown and a window of the Royal carriage was broken. Wake, a journeyman printer from Gosport, was tried by the court of King's Bench in February 1796 and was found guilty of a high misdemeanour in having 'indecently and disloyally hissed and hooted His Majesty' and in throwing a stone.

Sentencing was deferred until May, when Wake was given five years' hard labour in Gloucester Penitentiary (chosen because it had separate cells – ideal for state prisoners). Also, within the first three months of his sentence, he was to be stood in the pillory in a Gloucester street, on a market day. He also had to find sureties of £1,000 for his good behaviour for ten years after his release. In 1799, a poster was produced protesting against solitary confinement, with an illustration of Kidd Wake in his prison uniform. Wake was released in May 1801, having served his sentence and paid his sureties. (Whiting, J.R.S., *Prison Reform in Gloucestershire, 1776-1820*, 1975)

July 23rd

1904: A new Nurses' Home for the Gloucester Infirmary opened. The new building was sited, with a view to future extensions, on a portion of the Infirmary garden, adjoining Parliament Street. Two sections had been built so far, and space had been left for another wing to be added, if needed in the future.

The opening ceremony was supposed to take place on the lawn, but the weather was bad, so the Outpatients Hall of the Infirmary was used instead. The Right Hon. Sir Michael Hicks Beach, the Lord High Steward, performed the opening ceremony. Dignitaries who attended included Bishop Ellicott, the Mayor (Alderman Blinkhorn) and the City and County High Sheriffs. (*The Citizen*)

———— • ◆ • ————

1938: The foundation stone was laid at Gloucester's new church, St Oswald's, Coney Hill. The stone was laid by the Freemasons of the Province of Gloucestershire, with Masonic ceremony. Twenty-one officers of the Provincial Grand Lodge occupied the dais along with the Bishop of Gloucester (who dedicated the stone), the Rural Dean, and the vicar of Coney Hill, Revd P. McConnell. The Mayor and Corporation attended the ceremony. The new church was needed because of the rapid development of housing in Coney Hill. It was designed to seat 475 people. (*Cheltenham Chronicle*)

JULY 24TH

1788: King George III, the Queen, the Princess Royal and Princesses Augusta and Elizabeth, visited Gloucester, while staying at Cheltenham. They arrived at about 11 o'clock in the morning, amidst a general peel of church bells. The streets were lined with people who had come to greet them. At the Bishop's Palace, the party was received by the Bishop and his wife, Mrs Halifax, as a band struck up *God Save the King*. An address was made by the Bishop, who was attended by the Dean and the clergy of the Cathedral and city. Following this, the Mayor and Corporation were introduced.

After these formalities, the party looked round the Cathedral, then went to the pin factory of Messrs Weaver and Jefferis, followed by a visit to the Infirmary. The King presented £50 to the Bishop, who was the president of the Infirmary charity. After that, the party went to view the new prison, then under construction, where the builder, Thomas Cooke, showed them the plans. Everyone then returned to the Bishop's Palace, where they took refreshments, before setting off for Cheltenham again at about four o'clock. During the visit, the King was accompanied by the Bishop, the Mayor, the Duke of Norfolk, John Webb, Esq., and Alderman Weaver. The Queen was attended by Mrs Halifax. On the following Sunday morning, the Royal Family returned to Gloucester, to attend divine service at the Cathedral. (*Gloucester Journal*)

JULY 25TH

1789: John Price of Barton St Mary appeared before Justice of the Peace Mr Hayward, for swearing. Hayward may have experienced a feeling of *deja vu*, as Price had appeared before him previously, in April the same year, charged with the same offence. (*Calendar of Summary Convictions at Petty Sessions, 1781-1837*, ed. I. Wyatt, Gloucestershire Record Series, Volume 22, 2008)

———•◆•———

1942: The *Gloucester Journal* announced that this was the start of the holiday season, and this year, because of the war, everyone would be holidaying at home. Schools were going to stay open in order to look after children whose parents were working, or indeed to give any harassed housewives a rest. Teachers were going to take it in turns to supervise the activities.

There was to be 'a fortnight of gaiety' in Gloucester, in its parks and open spaces and in any public halls which weren't in use for war purposes. In a variety of ways, an effort was being made to bring the atmosphere of the seaside to those who couldn't go to the coast themselves. The obligation to stay at home for the holiday month offered an opportunity to go out and 'possess the land', yield to its attractions and share in its delights. (*Gloucester Journal*)

JULY 26TH

1870: Gloucester City Quarter Sessions took place in Shire Hall. While the County Quarter Sessions usually tried scores of prisoners, the City Sessions often only offered up one or two prisoners, or none at all. On this occasion, the city calendar was unusually busy, as there were five prisoners for trial.

Ann Winters and Mary Ann Baylis were found guilty of obtaining goods or money under false pretenses, and an old man named Robinson was acquitted of theft. The remaining two cases were more interesting. Herbert Taylor, a 25-year-old clerk, was sentenced to six weeks' hard labour, to begin when a sentence he was already serving had expired. He had gone to a Gloucester solicitor named Bretherton and said he had been sent from London to tell him his son, who lived in the capital, had broken his leg. Mr Bretherton gave Taylor refreshments, 15 shillings for his return railway fare and a blanket for the journey. When his wife went to London by the next train, it was discovered that the story was false.

Frederick Hardinge, a young carpenter, was sentenced to six weeks in prison for an assault upon Richard Matthams, a clerk. Believing Matthams and some friends had broken a window in the house where he lodged, as they walked home in the early hours of Christmas morning, Hardinge had thrown Matthams down, breaking his leg. (*The Citizen*)

JULY 27TH

1891: Henry Irving and Ellen Terry appeared at the Theatre Royal in Westgate Street, as part of its centenary year celebrations. They had arrived the previous night at the Bell Hotel, accompanied by Bram Stoker, acting manager at Mr Irving's London theatre, the Lyceum, and Mr Loveday, the stage manager. On this night, Irving performed in the tragic play, *The Bells*, and Miss Terry was in a comedy, *Nance Oldfield*. On the next evening, a banquet was held for the company at the Bell Hotel. They left the city on July 29th. (*Gloucester Journal*)

———— •◆• ————

1927: A lorry laden with 80 gallons of oil came into collision with an electric standard in London Road. The vehicle belonged to the Anglo-American Oil Company Limited, and was being driven by John Longdon, of Bristol. As it was passing under the railway bridge, the lorry skidded on the greasy surface of the road and crashed into the standard, crushing the casing. The front of the vehicle was badly damaged, but the driver was unhurt. (*The Citizen*)

July 28th

1884: The annual outdoor treat for the children attending the Whitefield Memorial Sunday school was held. The children assembled at the schoolroom at two o'clock, and were conveyed in covered vans to a field at Coney Hill, kindly lent for the occasion by Mr Thomas Long. The weather was not good, but the best was made of things. Tea was served under a large tent, and afterwards various amusements took place, with a number of prizes being distributed for races and other competitions. The party was accompanied to and from the field by the Whitefield Drum and Fife Band. The children returned home at about nine o'clock in the evening. (*The Citizen*)

July 29th

1901: At the Midland Railway Station, a Bristol train arrived in the afternoon carrying fourteen prisoners, wearing the usual broad-arrowed uniform, handcuffed, and secured together by a long chain. They were conducted by warders to an omnibus and driven to Gloucester Gaol. The newspapers commented that it was not the first occasion in recent times that Gloucester, with its roomy accommodation, had been used like this to relieve the strain on other prisons. (*The Citizen*)

1936: Film stars Miss Ann Harding and Miss Hedda Hopper spent the night at the New Inn in Gloucester. When she arrived, Miss Harding was wearing dark glasses and hid her face as she went into the hotel. She kept to her room until early the next day, to avoid being seen by the other guests. She said she was on a holiday tour of cathedral cities in England. (*Cheltenham Chronicle*)

July 30th

1862: Gloucester Park held an agricultural show, on the day it was formally opened to the public. A display of livestock, wheat, cheese and implements, and a horticultural exhibition took place in the park, and the proceedings were enlivened by the bands of the Grenadier Guards, the Gloucester City Rifles and the Artillery and Engineers. During the day, the park, which had been constructed on the old Spa grounds, was dedicated to the public forever, as a pleasure ground for the people. (*Western Daily Press*)

❖

1816: The Duke of Wellington visited Gloucester, to receive the Freedom of the City. He was welcomed by joyful shouts and cheers by an immense crowd of people, who were only prevented from taking the horses from the Duke's carriage and pulling it themselves at the sincere request of his Grace. The procession moved to the Tolsey, where the Corporation received him, and the Mayor presented him with the Freedom of the City. After the ceremony, the Duke and the Bishop of Gloucester, accompanied by a large party, walked to the spot where the National School was to be erected, and his Grace laid the foundation stone. The party then went to the King's Head Inn, where a sumptuous dinner was served. At about eight o'clock, the Duke left the party and took tea with the Bishop, before setting off for Cheltenham, where he was staying. (*Hereford Times*)

JULY 31ST

1535: John Falkner, the Mayor of Gloucester, rode out with a party of city dignitaries to greet King Henry VIII and his then wife, Ann Boleyn, who were coming to stay in Gloucester, after visiting Tewkesbury. On the following day, Falkner presented the King with ten fat oxen and other gifts. The royal couple stayed at Gloucester for four days, riding out into the countryside during the day and returning to the city in the evening. (Fosbrooke, T.D., *An Original History of the City of Gloucester*, 1819)

———◆———

1904: A longboat laden with hundreds of bags of maize and barley sank in the dock basin, opposite the warehouse of Messrs Philpotts and Co., corn merchants. The boat had been fine at four o'clock in the morning, when the nightwatchman passed it, but two hours later, it was seen disappearing below the water. Two longboats were placed on either side of it and four baulks of timber laid across them, and with the aid of crab winches and chains, the boat and cargo were quickly brought to the surface. The bags of grain were carried off by twenty-five to thirty workmen. The grain was consigned to Messrs Priday, Metford and Co., and Messrs Philpotts and Co., and after it had been landed on the quay wharf, prompt measures were taken to entail the least possible loss. (*The Citizen*)

AUGUST 1ST

1881: This was a Bank Holiday Monday, and one of the most prominent parts of Gloucester's programme of entertainments was the holding of a gala festival in Longford Park. The promoters were the employees of the Midland and the Great Western Railway Companies, who were raising funds for the Railway Servants' Orphanage at Derby. Mr Robinson had kindly given the committee permission to use part of his park – 30 to 40 acres in extent. The committee had arranged for special trains to run from Hereford, Cardiff and Swindon, in order to bring people into Gloucester.

A procession paraded through the city to Longford Park, which was opened to the public in the afternoon. The procession was composed of a number of the company's employees and their children, who travelled in four wagons, accompanied by members of the Oddfellows and Foresters Friendly Societies, in their full regalia, and a band. At the park, there were performances by dancers and other artists, along with demonstrations of athletic sports, and fireworks. (*The Citizen*)

AUGUST 2ND

1831: Charles Cole of Quedgeley appeared before magistrates, charged with two offences committed at his licensed premises on July 20th. The first charge was that he had allowed unlawful games to be played, for which he was fined 45 shillings including costs. The second charge was that he had allowed the consumption of beer after 10 o'clock at night. He was fined 47 shillings including costs for this offence. (*Calendar of Summary Convictions at Petty Sessions, 1781-1837*, ed. I. Wyatt, Gloucestershire Record Series, Volume 22, 2008)

———◆———

1888: Tuffley and Whaddon Flower Show took place. There was a good attendance, but it would probably have been higher if bad weather had not been threatened for the afternoon. There was a thunderstorm and heavy rain, but it cleared up later, to the delight of those who were taking part in athletics and games in the field opposite the schoolroom.

The flower show was a good one, despite the wretched weather which had been experienced that summer. As well as the botanical displays, there was a display of jersey cattle, a refreshment tent and a band. (*The Citizen*)

AUGUST 3RD

1878: The Assizes for the County and the City began at Shire Hall, before Mr Justice Manisty. Before the trials began, the judge addressed the County Grand Jury. He congratulated the county magistrates for assembling in such numbers, but couldn't congratulate them on the calendar, as it contained the names of thirty-five prisoners to be tried. Numerous crimes had been committed in the county, and several were of a serious nature; crime had been rife. He also commented on the 'scandalous' manner in which the depositions had been forwarded to him and complained that an incomplete calendar, containing the names of only twenty-six prisoners, had been sent to him. He told the Clerk of Assize to find out who was to blame.

In addressing the City Grand Jury, his lordship's mood improved. He was able to say his duty was exceedingly light and exceedingly pleasant, as there was only one prisoner for trial. The absence of serious crime in the city spoke well for those in authority. (*The Citizen*)

AUGUST 4TH

1890: Gloucester Athletics Club held its annual fixture on this Bank Holiday Monday, having decided to depart from its usual custom of holding it later in the month. Large numbers of people with a free day, lovely weather, and a 50 per cent reduction in ticket prices all helped to attract a large attendance. The President this year was Sir W.F.G. Guise.

The events held were the 120 yard Flat Handicap (local), the 1 mile Bicycle Handicap (open), the 120 yard Flat Handicap (open), the one lap (352 yards) Flat Handicap for boys under 16, the one mile Safety Bicycle Handicap (local), the 440 yards Flat Handicap (open), the half mile Flat Handicap (local) the Three Miles Bicycle Handicap (open); the one lap (352 yards) Flat Handicap, the Tug of War (first prize five pairs of boots), the one mile Flat Handicap (open), and the one lap Obstacle Race (local).

After the races, Lady Guise presented the prizes. The first prizes ranged from two to ten guineas. (*The Citizen*)

AUGUST 5TH

1104: Following the death of Serlo, the first Norman abbot of Gloucester Abbey, Peter succeeded him on this day. Serlo had been chosen to be abbot by the King, William the Conqueror, but Peter was a member of the community, elected to be abbot by his fellow brothers. He had been a prior for eleven years.

Abbot Peter's main achievements were acquiring more donations of land, building a stone wall around the abbey, and filling the cloister with many beautiful books. (Wallander, D., *The History, Art and Architecture of Gloucester Cathedral*, 1991)

1907: The following appeared in the 'For Sale' columns of *The Citizen*:

- Donkey, very quiet, accustomed to children and Bath Chair, also a very good saddle and brown harness.
- Boat House, Canal side, Hempsted, late property of Mr. W. T. Clutterbuck, deceased.
- A portable engine (by Marshall, Sons and Co., Gainsborough), 8 horse-power, in good working condition. Also 2 trollies.
- Good Wheat Straw, string-tied, suitable for thatching.
- Tree of early pears, fit to pick.
- Football goal posts and nets, complete.
- 10 very strong, white, ferrets.
- A pedigree Tamworth boar, about 10 months old.

AUGUST 6TH

1886: The burial took place of the last member of Gloucester's old Jewish community. Miss Amelia Abraham of Southgate Street had died at the age of 95. The Abrahams had been resident in Southgate Street for about 200 years, and Miss Abraham died in the house in which she was born. Her father had been a dealer, travelling jeweller and money changer. The latter was a lucrative trade in the days when many foreign ships came into the docks. Mr Abraham had also been the rabbi in the synagogue, then held at Mercy Place. He was succeeded as rabbi by his son, Michael. Miss Abraham was the last of the old Jewish community which had once flourished in Gloucester. At one time, there had been a large community in Eastgate Street, and all the pawnbrokers in Gloucester had been Jews.

The funeral of Miss Abraham took place at the Jews' burial ground, at the back of St Michael's Schools. The occasion excited a good deal of interest from the public. Only a few of those present were allowed into the ground during the ceremony, but afterwards the door was opened and the crowd was admitted. (*Gloucestershire Chronicle*; *Gloucestershire Notes & Queries*)

AUGUST 7TH

1883: The opening of the Gloucester Conservative Club took place, in the presence of a large assembly of members. Sir Michael Hicks-Beach and Mr Yorke, MPs, were present. After a tour of the premises, Sir Michael declared the club open, and made a long speech, most of which consisted of criticising Gladstone and the Liberals. Mr Yorke then moved a resolution expressing confidence in the Conservative leaders, which was seconded by Mr Granville Baker. The members of the club then held their first general meeting, and elected a president, officers and a committee. Only those who were able to show their membership cards at the door were admitted.

The club building was only partially completed at this time. Constitution House occupied an exceptionally good position, with the main entrance facing onto Brunswick Road. It had formerly been used as a girls' school, but lately had been let as offices. A limited liability company had been formed for the purpose of establishing the club. Its object, as stated in its prospectus, was 'to combine all classes of Conservatives, to assist in the organisation of the Party, and to provide for its members opportunities of social intercourse and rational recreation'. (*The Citizen*)

AUGUST 8TH

1914: War had been declared on Germany on August 4th, and four days later, troops from Gloucester were heading for active service. The 3rd Battery (Gloucester), 1st South Midland Brigade of Field Artillery, under the command of Colonel Metford, left Gloucester on two trains, seen off by a large crowd at the station. Photographs in the *Cheltenham Chronicle and Gloucestershire Graphic* showed their departure and 'Gloustrians giving their men a splendid send-off'. A few days after this, the Gloucestershire Yeomanry, which had been billeted in Gloucester for a week, also set off for war service, their destination unknown. The Yeomanry was made up of troops from Gloucester, Cheltenham, Ledbury, Winchcombe and Monmouth. (*Cheltenham Chronicle and Gloucestershire Graphic*)

AUGUST 9TH

1601: Thomas Rich (later Sir Thomas) was baptised at St John the Baptist Church in Northgate Street. Sir Thomas died in 1667, and in his will he bequeathed his house in Eastgate Street and £6,000 for a Blue Coat School in Gloucester, which would educate twenty poor boys. The Blue Coat School – so-called because the pupils wore distinctive blue coats and caps – opened in 1668. It later became known as Sir Thomas Rich's School.

The original house in Eastgate Street was demolished and replaced by a new building on the same site, in the early nineteenth century. The school later moved to Barton Street, and its old building was converted to become the Guildhall. Sir Thomas Rich's made another move in 1964, going to a new site at Elmbridge Farm, Longlevens, where it remains to this day. (*A History of the County of Gloucester, Volume IV: The City of Gloucester*, ed. N.M. Herbert, 1988)

———— • ◆ • ————

1905: Lionel Kemp, a pupil at the Commercial Travellers School, rescued a boy from the River Severn at Wainlode, near Gloucester. He was later awarded the Royal Humane Society's certificate for his bravery. Kemp's mother lived at Oxford Road, Gloucester. (*The Citizen*)

AUGUST 10TH

1643: The Siege of Gloucester, a key event in the course of the English Civil War, began on this day. Bristol had fallen to the King's supporters on July 26th, and the Royalists' attention turned to Gloucester next. The King's troops began to arrive outside Gloucester on August 6th, and King Charles joined them on August 10th, making his quarters at Matson House. Heralds were sent to the city at 2 o'clock in the afternoon to read out a proclamation from Charles, ordering the city to surrender. After four hours, word was sent back to the King, refusing to do so. This was the start of a siege which continued until September 5th. Many buildings in the suburbs were destroyed, to help keep the enemy out. The city's ordeal ended when a relief force of parliamentary troops arrived from London.

The King's decision to concentrate his forces and all of his attention on Gloucester was crucial to his demise, as it left London to be taken over by the Parliamentarians. (Atkin, M. and Laughlin, W., *Gloucester and The Civil War: A City Under Siege*, 1992)

August 11th

1586: John Sandys, a Roman Catholic priest, was hanged, drawn and quartered at Gloucester. The year before, it had been made an offence for a Roman Catholic to be in Queen Elizabeth's Realms. Sandys, who was born in Lancashire, had worked as a tutor to the children of Admiral William Winter at Lydney. In 1583 he travelled to France, and in June of that year he was ordained as a Roman Catholic priest at Reims Cathedral. He then returned to Lydney, staying for two years before he was arrested. He was tried at Gloucester and found guilty of high treason.

The punishment of being hanged, drawn and quartered was always an ordeal, but Sandys suffered a particularly terrible end, being cut down from the noose while he was still fully conscious, and then struggling with the executioner, who used a rusty and jagged knife to cut his body open. Sandys was beatified by Pope John Paul II on November 22nd 1987.

On May 4th 2007, the Feast of the English Martyrs, the Right Revd Declan Lang, Roman Catholic Bishop of Clifton, unveiled two plaques outside St Peter's Church in Gloucester, commemorating the fact that between 1585 and 1601, seven Catholics were executed in Gloucester because of their religious beliefs. (www.newadvent.org; *The Citizen*)

August 12th

1799: A 'Wanted' notice appeared in the press, offering a ten guinea reward for the apprehension of Mary Steward, a prisoner who had escaped from the City Gaol. She had been sentenced to seven years' transportation at the City Assizes, for stealing lace from the shop of Mrs Bright, milliner, in Gloucester. Steward escaped from the gaol by making a hole below the window in her cell and letting herself down using sheets she had torn into strips and sewn together. The 'Wanted' notice described her as being aged 28, born in Scotland and a milliner by trade. At the time of her escape she was wearing stockings, a flannel undercoat, a black skirt, a night cap and a black bonnet, but no gown, stays or shoes. The reward was offered by William Dunn, the gaoler at the City Prison. (*Gloucester Journal*)

AUGUST 13TH

1666: Thomas Pury, a Gloucester alderman and a former Member of Parliament for the city, died. Pury was elected as the city's representative in the Long Parliament of 1640. When the Civil War broke out, he became a captain in the parliamentary army, and played an active role in the defence of the city during the 1643 siege. Pury was re-elected as one of the representatives of the city in the First Protectorate parliament. In 1659, he and his son, also called Thomas, raised an army of 300 men to defend Gloucester from a possible Royalist attack.

After the Restoration in 1660, Gloucester was punished for its support of the parliamentary cause, losing its status as a county 'inshire' and having its boundaries reduced, as well as seeing the city walls demolished. In 1662, many of the city's aldermen were replaced by men who were considered to be more supportive of Charles II. Thomas Pury resigned before he could be removed. (*A History of the County of Gloucester, Volume IV: The City of Gloucester*, ed. N.M. Herbert, 1988; Austin, R., 'The City of Gloucester and the Regulation of the Corporations', in *Transactions of the Bristol and Gloucestershire Archaeological Society*, Volume 59)

AUGUST 14TH

1815: A dinner was held for the Corporation of Gloucester at the King's Head Inn, hosted by the Duke of Norfolk, who had just been elected as Mayor for the second time. After the tablecloth was removed, and the company was enjoying itself greatly, one of the guests, Mr Merrett Stephens, fell from his chair while singing a song, and died. Naturally, this dampened the spirits of the guests, and the party broke up soon afterwards. It was rumoured in some quarters that Stephens had just sung the line, 'and fly unspoiled, to the gates of heaven', when he died. (*Morning Post*)

1837: Thinking well ahead, Bishop James Henry Monk nominated his son to be Chancellor of the Consistory Court of the Diocese of Gloucester, although Charles James Monk was only 13 years old at the time. Monk junior eventually became Chancellor in 1859, three years after his father died. He had served as deputy to the old Chancellor, the Revd Phillips, who held the post for twenty-nine years, until his death. Monk also served as a member of parliament for the city several times, and in 1859 he was accused of using corrupt election practices, but did not lose his seat (see September 26th). Monk remained as Chancellor until 1885. (Gloucestershire Archives, Diocesan Records, 1541-2009, Appendix VIII, 'Chancellors of the Diocese'; *The Citizen*)

August 15th

1888: The death occurred of Mrs Jesse Sessions, at Teignmouth, where she and her husband, Alderman Sessions, were staying for the benefit of their health. She died two days before her 75th birthday. Mrs Sessions had been instrumental in establishing the Home of Hope in Gloucester in 1873. The home helped girls who were 'destitute, friendless and fallen', and gave them training in domestic science to enable them to get jobs in service. After the home opened, Mrs Sessions acted as its superintendent. With her husband, she took an active interest in temperance work. Both were members of the Society of Friends.

The funeral took place in Gloucester three days after her death, the hearse being followed by a long procession of mourners. Mrs Sessions was laid to rest in the burial ground attached to the Friends' Meeting House at Greyfriars. The ceremony was performed according to the simple customs of the Society of Friends. (*The Citizen*)

AUGUST 16TH

1844: At Gloucester Petty Sessions, held at Shire Hall, Caroline Carey made a complaint against Elizabeth Clark for causing 'wilful damage, by destroying her bonnet'. The matter was settled between the parties a few days later, without resorting to the judgement of the court. (Gloucestershire Archives, Gloucester Borough Records, GBR/G4/M1/2)

———•◆•———

1952: A coroner's inquest was held in Gloucester to decide whether a hoard of coins, found by builders in Lower Westgate Street, was a treasure trove. The men had been working in the yard of a former inn, the Royal Oak, and one of them had found a coin under a floor of quarry tiles and cobbles. On the next day, he and his workmates spent their lunch hour digging, and found 140 coins. They showed them to the curator of the city museum, who took them to the police station.

The inquest was held by the City Coroner, Trevor Wellington, and the verdict was that the find was a treasure trove, and was therefore the property of the Queen. The coins would be sent to the British Museum to be sorted and valued. The earliest coin was a shilling from the time of Edward VI (1550-53), and the others dated from 1553-1660. This was the first such inquiry in Gloucester for many years. (*The Citizen*)

AUGUST 17TH

1945: A 19-year-old 'Bevin Boy' appeared before magistrates for leaving his job without permission. Ronald Dewick, of No. 48 Regent Street, Gloucester, told the court that he was fed up with the mines and would not go back. He said he wanted to be in the army and to fight for his country. The Chairman, Mr H.G. Norman, told Dewick that he was fighting for his country by coal-mining as much as he would be by being in the army. Dewick replied that since the Bevin Boys had been introduced into the mines, the output had gone down. Mr Norman said it was not the bench's job to decide on political matters. He hoped the time was coming when everyone would be free to do as they liked, but for now they had to do as they were told. If Dewick talked nicely to the National Service Officer, he might be able to do something for him, but in any case he had to do what he was told to do for just a bit longer.

Dewick was bound over for twelve months and ordered to pay five guineas costs. He was told that if he was directed to go back to the mines and did not go, that would be a breach of his recognisance and he might be sent to prison. (*Western Daily Press*)

AUGUST 18TH

1892: Following extremely close weather the day before, a distinct earthquake was felt in Gloucester and its neighbourhood, soon after midnight. The shock was felt by residents in Stroud Road, London Road, and Tuffley, and further afield, in Maisemore, Hartpury and Elmore. Shocks were also felt in Bristol and parts of Wales. (*The Citizen*)

———◆·———

1933: An inquest was held into the death of Laurence Edward Rudge, aged 55, of No. 17 Nelson Street, Gloucester, who collapsed and died while riding a pedal bike in Hopewell Street. A post-mortem had revealed that Rudge, who was an ex-soldier, had pieces of shrapnel and bone in his lung. The coroner told the members of the jury that they had to decide whether the old war wound was a contributory cause of death.

The jury returned a verdict in accordance with the medical evidence, adding that they were of the opinion that the presence of shrapnel in the deceased's lung contributed to his death. (*Cheltenham Chronicle*)

AUGUST 19TH

1899: Captain Howard Blackburn arrived at Gloucester Docks in the evening, having made a single-handed voyage on a 30-foot vessel, the *Great Western*, across the Atlantic from Gloucester, Massachusetts. He had set sail on Sunday, June 18th and the journey had taken him sixty-one days. His feat was all the more remarkable because he had lost most of his fingers to frostbite, as well as several toes and the heel of his right foot.

Blackburn arrived at Kingroad on August 18th and stayed there for the night. The next day he took on board a pilot, Frank Price, who guided him up the Severn to Sharpness Docks. The SS *Sabrina* was in port there and offered Blackburn a tow along the canal to Gloucester. No formal reception had been organised at Gloucester, because it wasn't known on what day Blackburn would arrive. The Mayor was away on holiday, but the Deputy Mayor, the City High Sheriff and several prominent citizens, as well as a cheering crowd, were at the dock basin to greet him. He was conveyed in an open carriage to the Guildhall, where addresses were made to him, and he gave the Deputy-Mayor a letter from the Mayor of Gloucester, Massachusetts. Blackburn was invited to join the party for supper, but he said he wanted to get back to his boat. He stayed in Gloucester for a few days. (*The Citizen*)

August 20th

1871: The choir of Gloucester Cathedral re-opened on this Sunday, having been closed for three years. It had been renovated at a cost expected to be in the region of £13,000. The original estimate for restoring the whole Cathedral had been £10,000.

The walls had been thoroughly cleaned and repaired, and the floor had been lowered and re-laid with encaustic tiles. Old pews and reading desks had been replaced with handsome oak sittings, and the vaulted roof and its tracery had been made brilliant with gold and pigment.

At the services held on this day, the nave was crowded with citizens and visitors. A collection was taken after each service. The preacher in the morning was the Bishop, who took for his text the words of Isaiah, 'Our holy and beautiful house'. (*Cheltenham Looker-on*)

AUGUST 21ST

1896: An accident occurred at Gloucester railway station, in the Great Western Railway sheds, which resulted in a fatality. A fireman somehow lost control of an engine which ran into another engine and a van; these were driven by the impact over some stop blocks at the end of the shed and into the wall of an adjoining mess room, where five cleaners were eating breakfast. One of them, 16-year-old Frank Bourne, was just coming out of the door, and, being struck on the head by the van, was decapitated. His head was later found among the debris. Another worker was hit by falling brickwork, and a youth who tried to jump on the runaway engine to shut off the steam, slipped on the steps and narrowly escaped injury. (*The Citizen*)

AUGUST 22ND

1687: King James II visited Gloucester. He arrived at about five o'clock in the afternoon, having travelled from Bath. The King was met about two miles out of the city by the Bishop of Gloucester and members of the clergy, who escorted him on the remainder of his journey. At the South Gate, he was greeted by the Mayor and Magistrates in their robes, on horseback. The party then rode to the Cathedral, their route being lined by cheering crowds. The water conduits were running with wine, and all the church bells rang. The Dean and Prebends met King James at St Edward's Gate and escorted him to lodgings at the Dean's House, where he spent the night. (*The London Gazette*)

———— • ◆ • ————

1749: An advertisement appeared in the *Gloucester Journal* for the exhibition of a mermaid, who had apparently been captured off the coast of Mexico. She was appearing for two days at the New Inn. (*Gloucester Journal*)

AUGUST 23RD

1849: William Ernest Henley was born in Westgate Street, Gloucester. A pupil at the Crypt Grammar School, he became a poet, critic and editor, who introduced the early work of many great British writers of the 1890s to the public. Due to tuberculosis of the bone, which he developed when he was 12 years old, he had to have a leg amputated. In 1873, he went to the Edinburgh Infirmary, supervised by Joseph Lister, in an attempt to save his other leg, which succeeded. While there, Henley met Robert Louis Stevenson and the two became great friends. It is believed that Stevenson based at least a part of the character of Long John Silver in *Treasure Island* on his friend. (*Encyclopedia Britannica*)

———— • ◆ • ————

1841: The Girls' British School opened in Gloucester, four months after the Boys' School. The British Schools were partly funded by a government grant. Both sexes were to receive instruction in reading, writing, mental and slate arithmetic, English grammar, and general and scriptural history. In addition, the girls were to spend a portion of each day learning 'useful needlework'. (*Bristol Mercury*)

AUGUST 24TH

1580: John Taylor, known as the 'Water Poet', was born in Gloucester. He was sent to the Crypt School, but had difficulty with his Latin, so he was apprenticed to a London waterman. He was subsequently press-ganged into the Royal Navy, in which he served under the Earl of Essex. On retiring from the navy with a bad leg, Taylor became a waterman on the Thames. He took to making up rhymes to supplement his income, and acquired numerous patrons. Taylor eventually became a publican in London. He died in 1653, and was buried on December 5th at St Martin-in-the-Fields. (*Oxford Dictionary of National Biography*)

———— • ◆ • ————

1864: Gloucester was anticipating an execution, after Lewis Gough had been condemned to death at the recent assizes for murder. The authorities tried to keep the date of the execution secret, not wanting to attract a big crowd. This only fuelled the curiosity of the public, who kept a close look-out for the erection of the scaffold on the prison-lodge roof, and for the appearance of the famous hangman, William Calcraft. On this day, a white-bearded gentleman, who was walking down Westgate Street in the direction of the prison, was mobbed by a crowd, which mistook him for the executioner. The execution actually took place on August 27th. It was the last public hanging in Gloucester. (Evans, J., *Hanged at Gloucester*, 2011)

AUGUST 25TH

1739: Charles Wesley, Methodist preacher and hymn-writer, preached in Gloucester. He had sent a note to a minister asking to 'borrow the church', but received the reply that although the clergyman would be glad to have a glass of wine with him, he would not dare to lend him his pulpit for fifty guineas. Instead, Wesley preached in a field belonging to his friend George Whitefield. He spoke for an hour and a half to a crowd of about 1,000 spectators – far more than would have fitted in the church. (*The Journal of the Rev.Charles Wesley, M.A.*, ed. J. Telford, 1909)

August 26th

1805: The *Gloucester Journal* reported that William Evans, a private belonging to the 96th Regiment of Foot, stationed in the city, dropped down dead in Bull Lane. The coroners inquest returned a verdict that he died 'by Visitation of God'. (*Gloucester Journal*)

———◆·◆———

1816: Shire Hall, designed by Sir Robert Smirke, opened in Westgate Street, beside the old Booth Hall. The new building replaced its neighbour as the administrative headquarters of the county council. In the front part of the building, entered via a handsome columned portico, were a grand jury room, an office for the clerk of the peace, and a large function room, for the use of the public. At the back, there were two semi-circular courtrooms, in which were held the courts of Quarter Sessions and Assize.

Extensions took place in 1896 and 1910-11, to accommodate the increasing number of staff needed to run the council. In 1957, the old Booth Hall was demolished, to make way for a sizeable extension, which was built in the early 1960s. (*A History of the County of Gloucester, Volume IV: The City of Gloucester*, ed. N.M. Herbert, 1988)

AUGUST 27TH

1906: *The Citizen* carried notices for the Gloucester United Schools (which were the Girls' High School, the Crypt Grammar School, and Sir Thomas Rich's School), in anticipation of the new term, which was to start in September.

The Girl's High School, then situated at Bearland House, offered a course of instruction, which included English, Religious Knowledge, French, Latin, Mathematics, Science, Drawing, Drill, Needlework and Singing. Pupils were successfully prepared for the Cambridge Local Examinations. Three International Scholarships were awarded each year, which exempted pupils from tuition fees. The Headmistress, Miss Barwell, BA (London), would be at the school on the afternoon of Saturday, September 8th, to enter new pupils.

Sir Thomas Rich's School, then in Barton Street, announced that the Headmaster would be at the school on Saturday, September 8th, to enter new pupils and to receive the fees. Subjects here included Mathematics, French, Latin, Shorthand, Magnetism and Electricity, Chemistry, Drawing and Book-keeping. Sports included cricket, gymnastics, and swimming.

The Crypt School did not list its subjects, but informed readers that it had Classical, Modern and Junior departments. The latter was for boys aged 8 to 10. Fees were £5 per year, including the use of all printed books. The Townsend Scholarship, at Pembroke College, Oxford, consisting of £80 a year, with rooms, for four years, was attached to the school. (*The Citizen*)

AUGUST 28TH

1890: Ivor Gurney, composer and poet, was born in Gloucester. He was the son of a tailor, David Gurney, and his wife, Florence. Ivor was baptised on September 24th at All Saints' Church, where his uncle, Joseph Gurney, was the organist. He went to the National School in Gloucester, then in 1900 won a chorister's scholarship to the King's School. In 1906, he was articled to the organist of Gloucester Cathedral, Herbert Brewer, and in 1911 he won a scholarship to the Royal Academy of Music in London.

During the First World War, Gurney was wounded and gassed. Returning to Gloucester after the war, he suffered from severe depression. When he had recovered sufficiently, he went back to London to continue at the Royal Academy of Music, where he studied with Ralph Vaughan Williams.

In 1922, Gurney went to live with an aunt at Longford, then stayed at his brother's house in the city. In September 1922, he was certified insane and admitted to Barnwood House mental hospital. Later, he was transferred to another hospital in Dartford, Kent. Ivor Gurney died of tuberculosis on December 26th 1937. He was buried at Twigworth. (*Chambers Biographical Dictionary*; www.living-gloucester.co.uk)

AUGUST 29TH

1884: At a Town Council Meeting, the clauses of the bye-laws regarding the use of velocipedes (bicycles and tricycles) in the city were finalised, before being sent to the Local Government Board for approval. The main provisions were: velocipedes should not be used on the pavements; every rider should use a lamp between sunset and sunrise; every rider should carry a bell and give warning of his approach before passing any vehicle or passenger; every rider should observe the ordinary rules of the road, and every rider should dismount if riding the velocipede might frighten a horse or other beast. A fine of £2 would be payable for breaking any of these rules. The bye-laws came into force in October of that year. (*The Citizen*)

AUGUST 30TH

1752: Martin Benson, Bishop of Gloucester from 1735, died. Born on April 23rd 1689, in Herefordshire, Benson was nominated to be Gloucester's Bishop in January 1735. At that time, Gloucester was one of the poorest bishoprics in the country, but Benson declared his intention never to accept a higher preferment. During his time as Bishop, he carried out a survey of all the parishes in his diocese, noting what each was worth, the number of dissenters there, etc. He also made repairs to the Cathedral and the Bishop's Palace. Bishop Benson was buried on September 15th, in the Cathedral. (*Oxford Dictionary of National Biography*)

AUGUST 31ST

1888: At the City Petty Sessions, William Reed and Thomas Fletcher were summonsed under the Public Health Act, for throwing fish offal into Tabby Pitt's Pool. Both boys pleaded guilty. The Great Western Railway Company owned the land in Priory Road on which this pool was sited. It was in the process of filling it in, because of accidents, pollution and anti-social behaviour which took place there.

William Ponting, a railway servant, spoke of finding about a hundredweight of stinking fish in the pool. The two boys said they were sent there by their employer, Mr Maule, of Gloucester Fish and Game Supplies. The case was adjourned for a fortnight, to allow Mr Maule to appear.

On September 28th, Mr Maule appeared and said he had told the boys to take the fish to the pool, but to bury it. He thought it was unfair that Corporation workmen removed other fishmongers' putrid fish, but not his. Mr Blakeway, for the Corporation, said if the workmen had done so it was not with the permission of the Corporation. The boys were each fined one shilling plus costs. The money, which came to £1 in total, was paid by Mr Maule. (*The Citizen*)

SEPTEMBER 1ST

1939: With the news that Germany had invaded Poland, evacuations of children from large cities began. Gloucester received children from Birmingham, who began to arrive by train in the morning, met by crowds of spectators. The first train was expected to deliver over 800 children, but only 245 arrived. Stories circulated that some mothers had changed their minds about sending their children at the last minute. The children, with their labels attached to their clothes, left the station quietly but cheerfully, and most walked to the two schools from where they were distributed to the people who had promised to take them in. Pupils from a girls' secondary school which was twinned with Denmark Road School went there, while another twinned girls' school went to Linden Road.

The second train held 330 youngsters, including some who were very young – tiny children carrying bags or haversacks and their gasmasks. They were transported by coach, mostly to Longlevens. The third train to arrive at Gloucester contained grammar school pupils. There were 219 girls instead of the 380 expected, and 260 boys instead of the expected 360. The boys were taken to Sir Thomas Rich's School and the girls to Ribston Hall. (*The Citizen*)

September 2nd

1483: King Richard III granted a Charter to Gloucester by Letters Patent, by which it became 'the county of the town of Gloucester', and was administered independently from the county of Gloucestershire. The Mayor, who was chosen each year from among the aldermen, was to carry out the duties of clerk of the market, steward and marshall within the new county. A common council was formed, consisting of forty members, made up of the Mayor and the other eleven aldermen, two sheriffs, four stewards, and twenty-two other burgesses. The council had the right to hold their own courts and issue bye-laws, and were responsible for the maintenance of buildings, streets, etc., the preservation of order and the regulation of trade. The city's boundaries were extended to include the hundreds of Dudstone and King's Barton. (Wallander, D., *The History, Art and Architecture of Gloucester Cathedral*, 1991)

SEPTEMBER 3RD

1541: Following Henry VIII's dissolution of the monasteries, the diocese of Gloucester was created out of the medieval diocese of Worcester. The Abbey of St Peter became a cathedral, dedicated to the Holy Trinity. The former abbot of Tewkesbury Abbey, John Wakeman, became the Cathedral's first bishop, while the prior of St Oswald, Gloucester, became the first dean. Bristol was included in the new diocese at first, but in 1542 it became a separate see. Gloucester diocese did not enjoy autonomy for long, however, as in 1552 it was dissolved and combined once more with Worcester, because the revenues at Gloucester were too small to support a Bishop. Gloucester was separated from Worcester again in 1554, but from 1562, one Bishop held the sees of Gloucester and Bristol together. This continued until the holder resigned Bristol in 1589. Gloucester was then an autonomous see until 1836, when it was combined with Bristol once again. The two sees were not separated again until 1897. (*Fasti Ecclesiae Anglicanae, 1541-1837, Volume 8*, ed. J.M. Horn, 1996)

September 4th

1879: A cricket match took place at the Spa ground between Gloucester and a public schools' eleven, which was captained by Mr H.D. Kitcat. The weather was good, and the condition of the wicket was excellent. The visitors won the toss and elected to bat. Their last wicket fell just before lunch, with a total score of 112 runs. Mr Kitcat contributed 5 runs. On the next day, the match was decided on the first innings, in favour of Gloucester, who scored 142 runs. Kitcat took one wicket. (*The Citizen*)

***

1953: *The Citizen* announced on its front page that Blinkhorns, the well-known Gloucester drapers and furnishers, had been sold to F.W. Woolworth and Company Limited. Blinkhorns was one of the oldest businesses in Gloucester, having been carried on for many years, formerly by members of the Blinkhorn family. At this time it was owned by the John Lewis Partnership. There was also a Blinkhorns in Stroud, and John Lewis announced that both shops were to cease trading on September 19th. (*The Citizen*)

September 5th

1895: A branch of the Young Man's Christian Association (YMCA) was inaugurated in Gloucester, opened by Sir George Williams, the founder of the movement. The branch committee had bought and converted Greyfriars House as the Association's base. The property consisted of a large entrance hall, with stairs leading to the first floor. To the right of the hall was a meeting room, with a table laid out with newspapers and periodicals, a small writing table, and some armchairs. To the left of the hall was a lecture room, with the Secretary's office and a library behind it. Upstairs, there was a members' parlour and a small games room, and a lavatory and bathroom.

At the formal opening, the President of the Gloucester Young Man's Christian Association presented a silver key to Sir George Williams. He opened the door and led the company in a tour of the building. A short meeting was then held in the lecture room, followed by tea in the members' parlour.

The Gloucester YMCA left Greyfriars House in 1899, and a series of moves to different premises followed, until the branch settled in 1931 at No. 1 Brunswick Square. (*The Citizen; Gloucester Journal,* 1945)

September 6th

1881: An inquest was held at Messrs Ashbee & Co.'s timber yard, on the body of Charles Cates, who was drowned in the Gloucester & Berkeley Canal. Cates was 24 years old and a cabinet-maker, employed at Ashbee's.

On Sunday, September 5th, Cates and his two friends, John Vaughan and Charles Batten, hired three canoes at Priday's boathouse, and set off down the canal. When they got to the gas works, Batten's canoe capsized. Vaughan helped him out, while Cates, who could not swim, tried to rescue Batten's hat, and fell into the water. Batten tried to paddle over to help, but capsized again and had to be fished out. A man passing on a longboat threw a line to Cates three times, but he didn't manage to grab it. A group of men were standing on the bank, and one of them got on a raft and held out a boat hook, but Cates couldn't reach it. He finally disappeared under the water and did not resurface. His body was found later that day.

The Coroner warned against people who could not swim using canoes on the canal, where the water was very deep. The boatman at Priday's had asked the three friends if they could swim, and they all said they could. The jury returned a verdict of accidental death, and gave their fees to Cates's widow. (*The Citizen*)

September 7th

1784: An announcement in the local papers stated that races were to be run at Gloucester on this day, for a plate of £50. Entry was free for horses of all ages, and the winner would be the best over three heats of four miles each. On the same day, two sweepstakes were to be held of twenty guineas each, between Lord Sherbourne's horse, Glancer, Lord Surrey's Captain Tart, Captain Snell's Caroline and Mr Wheatley's Trinidad. (*Hereford Journal*)

———— • ◆ • ————

1941: During a National Day of Prayer service, the Bishop of Gloucester, Dr Headlam, stated that while the army was disciplined and patriotic, it was said that those employed in the factories were 'slacking', and cared only for the substantial amounts of money they earned. His words caused great offence, and a flurry of angry letters were sent to the local newspapers. Later in the month, a deputation of seven employees of the Gloster Aircraft Company Factory went to meet the Bishop at his Palace, where a full exchange of views took place.

The Bishop released a statement afterwards, saying that his comments were not an attack on munitions workers in particular; he had only been talking about a small number or workers, and his remarks were meant to apply to the slackness of the nation as a whole. The deputation said Dr Headlam had been very courteous. (*Gloucester Journal*)

September 8th

1935: Vast crowds gathered in King's Square to greet General Evangaline Booth of the Salvation Army when she visited Gloucester. General Booth was in the final stages of a tour of England, in which she visited forty towns.

At Gloucester, many people waited nearly an hour for the General's appearance. The City Salvation Army band played for half an hour before she arrived in King's Square, escorted by the Mayor, the City High Sheriff and other dignitaries, and was greeted by an outburst of public enthusiasm. She made a striking figure in her symbolic red coat and hat. Thousands stood for thirty minutes in King's Square, listening in intense silence to the General's words, which ended on a note of tremendous religious fervour – many in the audience had tears running down their cheeks.

After leaving Gloucester, General Booth went on to Cirencester and Swindon. (*Gloucester Journal*)

SEPTEMBER 9TH

1890: Match girls employed at Moreland's Match Factory in Bristol Road went on strike. The girls wanted an increased rate of pay, and the refusal of their employers to offer them more money resulted in a walk-out. The cause of the match girls was taken up by other trades in the city, and a deputation from their various unions was sent to Moreland's to negotiate for a settlement. After a fortnight, the girls returned to work, having been offered a small pay rise; they were to be paid one shilling for every thirteen boxes filled, rather than the previous rate of one shilling for fourteen boxes. Another result of the strike was that a branch of the Women's Trade Union was established in the city, which had 113 members by September 24th. (*The Citizen*)

September 10th

1874: The Mayor of Gloucester held a meeting at the Tolsey, attended by leading merchants and traders in the city, to finalise plans to set up a steamship company in Gloucester, in order to establish a regular line of steamers carrying goods between Gloucester and the ports of Ireland and France. More than half of the capital required had already been provided by private subscribers; the remaining shares were to be offered to the public. The Mayor suggested the formation of a limited liability company, a proposal which was favourably received. It was agreed that a company should be formed under the Limited Liability Acts to be called 'The Gloucester Steamship Company Limited', with a capital of £20,000 in 2,000 shares of £10 each. The amount of capital already raised was about £11,000.

In January 1875, it was reported to the Gloucester Board of Commerce that one steamship had been purchased. Notices in April advertised that the company's new Twin Screw steamer, *Henry Allen*, would soon commence travelling between Gloucester and Cork, carrying iron goods, merchandise and provisions, etc. In April 1876, the company was hoping to buy another boat, but by 1879, the company was making a loss and was eventually wound up. (*Bristol Mercury*)

September 11th

1741: A crowd of spectators watched a demonstration of the city's new fire engine – 'Mr Newsham's Fourth Size Engine'. It was supplied with water from the reservoir at Robinswood Hill. By use of its suction pipe, the water, by its own weight, raised itself in a column to the top of the High Cross, which was over 30 feet high. The *Gloucester Journal* commented that this meant 'the city could be provided for against the casualties of a fire, which is a great satisfaction and a blessing to the inhabitants thereof.' (*Gloucester Journal*)

1899: *The Citizen* carried an advertisement for Herbert & Sons, Corsetieres of Gloucester. They were the sole agents for the 'Transvaal' corset, which was 'specially suitable for slightly fuller figures'. It was a corset which would wear well, and, while showing off the figure to the best possible advantage, was perfectly comfortable. The 'Transvaal' corset was finished off below the bust by 'a deep band of firm but inelastic material, which effectually reduces the width of the figure while keeping the waist well in place'. The price of this wonderful garment was 6s 11d. (*The Citizen*)

SEPTEMBER 12TH

1826: William Cobbett arrived at Gloucester, having travelled for 25 miles, hoping to spend the night in the city. Unfortunately, he had arrived during the Three Choirs Festival, described by him as 'one of those scandalous and beastly fruits of the system, called a Music Meeting', where cathedrals were used as opera houses. In consequence, it was impossible to get a bed unless one was willing to 'bow very low and pay very high'. He moved on from 'this scene of prostitution and of pocket-picking' to spend the night at Huntley, but not before an ostler in Gloucester charged him nine pence for letting his horse stand for ten minutes, and abused him when he refused to give him a tip. (Cobbett, W., *Rural Rides*, 1830)

———•◆•———

1929: The Mayor officially opened Gloucester's new omnibus service, with the commencement of the Oval to Longford service. In his speech, the Mayor stated that the day of the tram had gone. The *Western Daily Press* published a photograph of one of the new buses passing the last tram on the Kingsholm route. The tramcar was decorated with a piece of black crêpe and carried a notice stating, 'A token of regret for the last tram. R.I.P.' The electric tramway had come to Gloucester in 1904, replacing the old system of horse-drawn trams. (*Western Daily Press*)

SEPTEMBER 13TH

1726: A Mr Rice arrived at Gloucester, having driven from Worcester in a chair drawn by four dogs. Due to recent heavy rain, the condition of the roads was very bad, but he arrived at the city at about 2 o'clock in the afternoon of the same day he had left Worcester. Mr Rice intended to stay in Gloucester for a short time, 'to gratify those who are lovers of Curiosity'. (*Worcestershire Chronicle*)

———◆———

1631: Accepted Frewen was installed as the Dean of Gloucester on this day, by proxy. He took his oaths in person on October 6th. He left Gloucester in 1643, when he was promoted to become Bishop of Lichfield and Coventry. Frewen's career prospered under King Charles I, who appointed him as one of his chaplains, but in 1652, Parliament forfeited his estates. Cromwell put a price on his head, but the proclamation called him 'Stephen Frewen', which gave him the opportunity to escape to France. After the Restoration, Frewen was appointed Archbishop of York. (*Oxford Dictionary of National Biography*)

September 14th

1528: John Cooke, co-founder of the Crypt Grammar School, died. In his will, he left money for his widow, Dame Joan, to start a grammar school in Gloucester. Dame Joan carried out her late husband's wish with great determination. In 1529, the prior of Llanthony Secunda, Richard Hart, made a grant of land to Joan Cooke, giving part of the graveyard of St Mary de Crypt to be used for a schoolhouse. Things moved slowly, however. Ten years after John Cooke died, Letters Patent were granted by Henry VIII, enabling the Mayor and Burgesses of Gloucester to accept manors, lands and rents to the value of £50 a year for the purpose, among others, of making and maintaining a grammar school.

In 1539, perhaps knowing that the St Mary de Crypt site would eventually be outgrown, Letters Patent were passed, sanctioning the purchase by Joan Cooke and her advisors of additional lands for the Crypt Grammar School, previously held by the dissolved Llanthony Priory. A receipt for £266 6s 8d was issued to Dame Joan Cooke for the endowment of the school, as provided by the will of John Cooke. These lands were at Podsmead, in the parish of Hempsted, where the school moved in 1862, and where it stands today. (Lepper, C., *The Crypt School, Gloucester, 1539-1989*, 1989)

SEPTEMBER 15TH

1884: Edwin Brown appeared in the Petty Sessions court, charged with maliciously damaging the door and window of his father John Brown's house, and also with using threats of violence towards him. The complainant stated that he had experienced a lot of trouble from the 'young gentleman'. His son had tried to force an entrance into his house and committed about 5 shillings' worth of damage to the window and door. He was afraid that his son would do him some bodily harm, for he had frequently used threats of violence against him.

Inspector Piff gave evidence in support of the charge. There was a long blacklist against the prisoner. Edwin Brown was ordered to pay 2s 6d and costs, plus 5s damages for the first offence, or spend seven days in prison, and for the second charge, he was to find two sureties of £15 each, and to be bound over in his own recognizances of £30 to keep the peace for six months, or, in default, serve three months in prison. The prisoner was taken into custody. (*The Citizen*)

September 16th

1901: Theodore Chambers, director of the British and Foreign Electrical Vehicle Company, in the course of his experimental tour with an electric motor car, came to Gloucester to get a recharge at the Gloucester Municipal Electric Lighting Works. The car had been driven from London to Glasgow, taking part in the trials at the London Exhibition, and held the record for the longest distance on one charge – 96½ miles. The vehicle, which weighed two tons, had run 3,000 miles since June, without a change of batteries. Mr Chambers said that the motion of the car was delightfully smooth, with little or no vibration or noise. (*The Citizen*)

SEPTEMBER 17TH

1823: The first day of the Three Choirs Festival began in Gloucester, in what was then regarded as its centenary year. The opening day of the 'Centenary Festival' was wet and unpleasant, yet the Cathedral was thronged for the service. A sermon was preached by the Revd Dr Timbrill, followed by a performance of Knyvett's *Coronation Anthem*. The concert in the evening, held at the Shire Hall, was attended by a very respectable audience.

The second day's performance at the Cathedral was also well attended, the audience being treated to a selection of favourite pieces from Handel's works. A bumper crowd attended the concert at Shire Hall in the evening. On the final day, the *Messiah* was performed in the morning. Despite fainting in the Cathedral, Miss Stephens, one of the soloists, managed to perform *I Know that my Redeemer Liveth* very well. Miss Stephens sang again at the evening concert, where a rendition of *God Save the King* closed that year's entertainment. (*Gloucester Journal*)

———◆———

1787: The following notice appeared in the *Gloucester Journal*:

> Wanted, in an airy situation, in (or within a mile of the city of) Gloucester, a small, convenient HOUSE in perfect repair, rent from 12 to 16 pounds per annum. – Address, by letter, to Mr Cook, builder, Gloucester. A House on the London Road preferred.

SEPTEMBER 18TH

1879: An accident occurred at Gloucester Docks, when a longboat sank. The *Providence* was lying alongside a French schooner on the canal, opposite the oil mill near Llanthony Bridge, with a cargo of salt, which was to be discharged into the schooner. The tarpaulins of the longboat had just been thrown back, when, either from the wash of the steamer *Lapwing*, which had just passed, or from some unknown cause, the water began to flow into the boat and it became evident that she was in danger of sinking.

The master, Richard Jones, went down into the cabin to fetch his money and watch before leaving the boat, but before he could get out, a rush of water caused it to sink. It proved impossible to rescue the captain, and he died. (*The Citizen*)

———◆———

1997: A memorial service was held in Gloucester Cathedral to commemorate the life of the Revd W.V. Awdry, the author of the *Thomas the Tank Engine* books, who had died earlier that year. Although he was not a native of Gloucestershire, Awdry had moved to the Stroud area in 1965, when he retired as a full-time minister. He often preached at Rodborough parish church. Among his many interests, he was an active member of the Gloucestershire Society for Industrial Archaeology. (*The Citizen*; www.gsia.org.uk)

SEPTEMBER 19TH

1821: A man was flogged at a cart's tail through the main streets of Gloucester, as part of his punishment for 'child-stealing'. He had taken five children in total, and had said that he had been employed to steal them, but would not reveal for what purpose. A huge crowd watched the punishment being inflicted, and the pin factory and other businesses were deserted. Most vociferous in their calls were the women, who complained that the prisoner was not being whipped hard enough. (*Freeman's Journal*)

1981: *The Citizen* reported that a mosque could be open in Gloucester within a year, now that detailed planning permission had been given for the building in All Saints' Road. The project entailed the demolition of the former warehouse where the city's Muslims had been worshipping for several years. The new mosque would be 'in the Eastern style', with a minaret and dome. The mosque, named *Jamia al Karim*, opened in 1985.

On September 23rd of the same year, *The Citizen* printed an article on the demolition of two houses in Ryecroft Street, which had also been used as a mosque by Muslims in Gloucester. A mosque was built on this site also, named *Masjid E-Noor*, which opened in 1983. (*The Citizen*; *A History of the County of Gloucester, Volume IV: The City of Gloucester*, ed. N.M. Herbert, 1988)

SEPTEMBER 20TH

1803: *The Times* reported that a Quaker had been committed to Gloucester gaol for three months by magistrates, for refusing to be sworn into, or provide a proper substitute for, the County Militia. (*The Times*)

———•◆•———

1893: A Harvest and Dedication Festival was held at Matson. A thanksgiving service for the gathering in of crops was held in the parish church, and as the nave was being rebuilt at this time, a dedication stone was laid. Because the nave was still open to the elements, the worshippers gathered under an improvised canvas roof.

At the conclusion of the harvest service, the Hon. Maria E.R. Rice laid a dedication stone in the west wall of the nave, to the loving memory of her sister, the Hon. Katherine S.R. Rice, daughter of the late George Talbot Rice, Baron Dynevor. A parchment in a bottle was placed beneath the stone, recording by whom, and in whose memory, the stone was laid. A short history of the church was also included. As the saint to whom the church had originally been dedicated was not known, it was now dedicated to St Katherine. The Revd William Bazeley declared the stone well and truly laid, the choir sang the hymn, *Christ is Our Corner-stone*, and the Benediction was pronounced. (*The Citizen*)

SEPTEMBER 21ST

1827: A riot broke out over the paying of tolls on Westgate Bridge. About a hundred workmen were engaged in building a new bridge at Over, and at night, when they finished work, they had to cross Westgate Bridge to enter the city. On this night, the workers refused to pay and when the toll-keeper's wife would not let them pass, they tore down the palings on one side and crossed without paying.

On September 25th the palings were repaired, and that evening the workmen were joined by bargemen and others, until, eventually, there was a crowd of about 1,000 men and women. The toll-gate was torn down and thrown into the river and the toll-house was virtually destroyed. On the following afternoon, two troops of dragoon guards arrived to maintain order, and three bargemen were arrested for their part in the riot. However, the bridge commissioners agreed to end charges on foot passengers within a few weeks of the riot, and by the end of 1828, tolls were no longer charged on Westgate Bridge. (*The Times*; *A History of the County of Gloucester, Volume IV: The City of Gloucester*, ed. N.M. Herbert, 1988)

———•◆•———

1945: The *Western Daily Press* reported that the Coronation Chair, which had been secretly stored at Gloucester Cathedral for the duration of the war, had been sent back to Westminster a few days previously. (*Western Daily Press*)

September 22nd

1899: At Gloucester Petty Sessions, Mr J. Malling, of the Robinhood Inn, Mr C. Radford, of the New Pilot Inn, and Mr A.A. Johnston, of the Llanthony Bridge Inn, renewed their application to make permanent a special license to open their houses at half past five in the morning, instead of the usual six o'clock, for the convenience of workers in their vicinities. They had previously been given permission to open early for three months, which was to be reconsidered on this day. In the case of the Robinhood Inn, a memorial had been signed by 400 men living in country districts around Gloucester, who had taken advantage of the earlier opening time during the last three months, and spoke of the great convenience of being able to get refreshments before six o'clock.

All the employers near the inns opposed the application. The foreman of Price, Walker and Co. said they had a mess room with tea and coffee provided all day, which opened at half past five in the morning. Since the new opening hours at the inns were introduced, some of the men did not come in to work until nine o'clock, and others didn't turn up at all. The Bench retired to consider the case, and decided not to grant the application. (*The Citizen*)

SEPTEMBER 23RD

1893: An inquest was held at the Ship Inn, the Quay, into the death of Charles Guy, whose body had been found in the water, near the Westgate Bridge. Guy was 25 years old and lived with his sister and brother-in-law at No. 100 St Catherine Street. Sydney Overthrow said he had been drinking on Saturday night with Guy in the Dean's Walk Inn. They left about eleven o'clock and were crossing St Catherine's Meadow, about 100 yards from the river, when they decided to have a sleep in the field. When Overthrow woke up, it was very foggy and he could not see his friend anywhere, so he went home, arriving at about half past one in the morning. Overthrow admitted to the Coroner that he and Guy may have been 'a little the worse for liquor', but that they were not incapable. He had been in bed with a bad cold since that night.

Samuel Priday, a boat-builder of the Nag's Head Inn, Westgate Street, had known the deceased well. He had found Guy's body on the previous day. Guy had been a very good oarsman and a member of the Gordon League Rowing Club, but unfortunately, he could not swim. The Coroner concluded that Guy had probably fallen into the river on that foggy night. A verdict of 'accidentally drowned' was reached. (*The Citizen*)

SEPTEMBER 24TH

1736: Robert Raikes, the eldest son of the founder of the *Gloucester Journal*, was baptised at St Mary de Crypt Church in Southgate Street. Born on September 14th, he was the eldest son of Robert Raikes senior. Robert junior took over the running of the *Gloucester Journal* in 1757, when his father died. He is perhaps best known for starting a Sunday school in 1784 with Thomas Stock, which was held in St Mary de Crypt Church. Raikes used his position as a newspaper proprietor to advantage, giving the Sunday School movement maximum publicity in his publication. He retired from the newspaper business in 1802. Robert Raikes junior died on April 5th 1811 and was buried in the church with which he had held a life-long association. (*Oxford Dictionary of National Biography*)

1880: Reverend Sir J. Hobart Culme Seymour, Senior Canon of Gloucester Cathedral and Chaplain to the Queen, died at the age of 81. He had been a canon at Gloucester for over fifty years. (*Lloyds Weekly*)

SEPTEMBER 25TH

1858: Newspapers reported that a Gloucester girl had been 'rescued from the Mormons'. According to the Utah correspondent of the *New York Herald*, an important law case had been heard in which Henry Polydore, of Gloucester, England, was the plaintiff, and Samuel W. Richards, a Mormon dignitary, and his fourth wife, Jane Mayer, were defendants. Polydore and his wife had separated a few years previously and their daughter, Henrietta, had been sent to a Roman Catholic boarding school in Lincolnshire. In 1854, when Henrietta was 8, Mrs Polydore had abducted the girl from the school and went to America with the Mormons.

The mother came back to England some time after this, leaving the girl with Mrs Polydore's sister, Jane Mayer, who had married Samuel W. Richards. Henrietta was still with her aunt four years later, and was now 12 years of age. Mr Polydore got to hear about his daughter's situation and determined to get her back. Henrietta, who had been called 'Lucy' in America, was the subject of a three-day hearing, which resulted in an order that she should be returned to her father in Gloucester. At the time of the report, she was in the custody of a US Marshal. (*Gloucester Journal*)

September 26th

1859: A Commission of Inquiry began in Gloucester into corruption during the last parliamentary elections in Gloucester. In 1857, William Philip Price and Charles Monk stood as Liberal candidates against Sir Robert Carden, the Conservative candidate. Price and Monk won by a healthy majority. However, a petition was soon got up requesting an investigation into the alleged bribery of voters. It was decided that there was not enough evidence against Monk, but Price was unseated while an inquiry was held.

This took place over four weeks, and detailed evidence about the level of bribery which had taken place at the election, not just on the part of the Liberals, but by the Conservatives too, was heard. Monk, who was the son of a former Bishop of Gloucester and the Chancellor of the Diocese, insisted that he knew nothing at all about bribes being given. The other two suggested that any bribery carried out by their managers was without their knowledge.

Mr Wilton, a Gloucester surgeon who canvassed on behalf of the Liberals, admitted to paying out nearly £1,000 in bribes and 'treats'. The Conservative canvassers had paid out about the same, but said they had been obliged to do so because of the amount of bribes being offered by their rivals. It was concluded that the bribery of voters was a common practice in Gloucester. (*Gloucester Journal*)

SEPTEMBER 27TH

1944: At their weekly meeting, the City Council decided to engage the Children's Theatre Company to perform in Gloucester's schools, thus reversing the decision taken by the Education Committee the previous week. At the Education Committee meeting, Alderman W.H.S. Colborn had presided, and his casting vote meant it had been decided not to allow the theatre company to perform in the schools this year, even though it had done so previously.

Colborn had said that drama represented life in a false light, and in his opinion, the stage and theatricals were among the most dangerous aspects of modern times. The excitement of films and drama caused mental sickness, and he was sure it was wrong to introduce tragedy to children. Mr Haines, who was in favour of booking the company, said he had seen some of their productions when they had last visited Gloucester, and that they were of special educational value and designed to fit in with schoolwork. Another councillor objected to the fee of £45 to book the company.

Colborn's remarks had excited a great deal of public comment, and the City Council's motion to reverse the decision was won by a majority of twenty-seven votes. Of the three members who opposed the motion, only Alderman Colborn spoke. He said he did not know that the work of the Children's Theatre Company was so far removed from the ordinary realm of drama. (*Gloucester Journal*)

September 28th

1882: Today was the first day of the annual Barton Fair, which consisted of a livestock sale held at the cattle market and a general funfair in Barton Street. It was reported that at the cattle market, the number of horses was larger than usual and sheep did well, but there were fewer cattle than on previous occasions. In Barton Street, there was a variety of booths and shows, with the inevitable shooting galleries and coconut booths. One novel feature this year was a curious display of boats and balloons. There was also a waxwork display sprawled across the streets in front of the railway gates. Another novelty this year was the presence of an 'iron-jawed man', advertised by an illustration showing him holding in his mouth a barrel, with three men sitting on it. (*The Citizen*)

SEPTEMBER 29TH

1849: Queen Victoria, Prince Albert and their children changed trains at Gloucester station. This was necessary because of the differences in gauge width between the Birmingham to Gloucester line and the Gloucester to Bristol line, which meant that everyone travelling between Birmingham and Bristol had to alight at Gloucester and cross a platform to change trains.

When the train drew in to the station just before noon, the Mayor, the sword-bearer and Revd Sir John Hobart Seymour were invited to approach the carriage and deliver their addresses on behalf of the Corporation and clergy. The Revd Sir John, as one of the Queen's chaplains, was allowed to kiss her hand. The Queen stepped from the narrow gauge carriage, bowed to the Mayor on passing him, and entered the state carriage of the Great Western Railway. Prince Albert, the Princess Royal, the Prince of Wales, Princess Alice and Prince Alfred hastened from one carriage to the other without pausing. The Corporation and clergy advanced to be presented to the Queen, but were followed by the ticket-holding spectators who had been behind them, causing a crush and pressing the dignitaries upon the Royal carriage and upsetting flowerpots. The Queen graciously presented herself at each side of the carriage. The party's luggage was left at Gloucester for the departure of the next train. The visit was over in about five minutes. (*Gloucester Journal*)

September 30th

1927: Frank Williams, a rag and bone dealer living in a caravan near Westgate Bridge, was charged at the City Petty Sessions with neglecting his wife and children, so they became chargeable to the Gloucester Poor Law Union. Williams had left the city in August and returned during the Barton Fair. He had been away for seven weeks, and his family had gone on parish relief.

Mr Armitage, Clerk to the Board of Guardians, prosecuted. He said that there were too many husbands who neglected to maintain their families, and it was unfair that ratepayers should have to maintain the families of men who deliberately went away to escape their responsibilities. Williams said that he did not want the Workhouse to maintain his family, and he went away to look for work. A relieving officer employed by the Gloucester Board of Guardians said Williams' wife and children had been chargeable to the Guardians many times over many years.

The prisoner told the magistrates that his trade was rag and bone collecting and he could not get enough of it to keep his children. He could name every town and factory he had been to in the last six weeks looking for work. He was sentenced to one month's hard labour. As he left the dock, he said to the Poor Law Union officials, 'Now you have to keep the children'. (*The Citizen*)

OCTOBER 1ST

1762: Mary Hopkins, a victualler, became the first woman to be registered as a Freeman of Gloucester. (*A Calendar of the Registers of the Freemen of the City of Gloucester, 1641-1838*, ed. J. Jurica, Gloucestershire Record Series, Volume 4, 1991)

1836: John Edwards and Elizabeth Harwood were charged on the oaths of two police officers with having been drunk and disorderly in the parish of St Nicholas. Edwards was also charged with assaulting one of the officers in the execution of his duty. Edwards was fined 20 shillings plus costs, which he immediately paid; Harwood was imprisoned for fourteen days, for being idle and disorderly, and a prostitute. (Gloucestershire Archives, Gloucester Borough Records, GBR/G4/M1/1)

1916: Richard Cummins Haine was born in the parish of St Stephen, Gloucester. He was educated at the Crypt School, then became an apprentice with the Gloster Aircraft Company. During the Second World War he joined the RAF and served as a pilot. He was awarded the Distinguished Flying Cross for his actions over Holland in 1944, where he was one of six Blenheim fighters of 600 Squadron ordered to attack the key airfield at Waalhaven. His was the only aircraft not to be shot down. Group Captain 'Dickie' Haine, as he was known, died in 2008. (*The Daily Telegraph*)

OCTOBER 2ND

1786: The *Gloucester Journal* commented that the number of people who had died within the last six months by going home from markets in a state of intoxication had been very considerable in the county. The latest victim was a farmer from Hartpury, returning home from Barton Fair one evening, who was so excessively drunk that he fell from his horse over the parapet of Westgate Bridge, into the Severn, and was drowned. His body was not found until the following night. (*Gloucester Journal*)

———◆———

1915: A procession made its way through Gloucester, with the intention of attracting people to work in the munitions factories, during the war. Most of the people in the procession were men from the Wagon Works, and Fielding and Platt Ltd; there were also some women workers. Floats were used to illustrate the work being done in the factories. (Voyce, J., *The City of Gloucester*, 1995).

OCTOBER 3RD

1903: About thirty-three employees of Fielding and Platt Ltd, of the Atlas Ironworks, gathered at the Bristol Restaurant in Gloucester to take part in a presentation to Mr Francis J. Platt, who was leaving the firm to become managing director of Dudbridge Iron Works, near Stroud. An apology had been sent from John Fielding, who had a previous engagement, so James Mercer, one of the foremen, presided.

Alfred Taylor, foreman of the pattern shop, presented Mr Platt with a handsome gold English lever watch. Mr Platt was told that all the workers regretted his departure. The old hands knew how happy relations were between them and Mr Platt's late father, Mr James Platt. In response, Mr Platt said he was deeply touched. He had been connected with the Atlas Ironworks all his life, and he saw some old faces there whose service with the firm went back thirty-five years. He asked the company to drink a toast of, 'Continued success to the Atlas Ironworks'. (*The Citizen*)

OCTOBER 4TH

1834: An advertisement appeared in the *Gloucester Journal*, inviting labouring men with families to apply for allotments, which were to be made available on ground at Kingsholm.

Interest in the allotment system had been growing nationally since the formation in 1830 of the Labourer's Friend Society, which wanted to improve the living standards of the poor, and widely promoted the benefits of the allotment system. The Bishop of Gloucester was appointed as the vice-president of the Labourer's Friend Society in March 1834.

The cause of the Labourer's Friend Society was helped by the patronage of King William IV, and by three Acts of Parliament, passed between 1831 and 1832, which enabled parishes to enclose up to fifty acres of wasteland and brown land for use as allotments. A number of parishes, particularly in the Stroud and Cirencester areas, had already established and let out allotments before Gloucester joined in with the scheme. (Loosley, J., 'Early Allotments in Gloucestershire', in *Archives & Local History in Bristol & Gloucestershire*, ed. J. Bettey, 2007)

OCTOBER 5TH

1807: The Prince of Wales (later George IV) made a visit to Gloucester, while he was staying at Berkeley. He was met at Hempsted by a military escort, which accompanied him into the city. At the Tolsey, the Corporation presented him with the Freedom of the City, and entertained him with a dinner at the King's Head Inn in Westgate Street. (*Gloucester Journal*)

———◆———

1929: The *Gloucester Journal* reported that 'one of the biggest and most important air industries in the British Isles' would shortly be established at works only ten minutes drive from Gloucester city centre. Up to 1,000 men would be employed there and would spend a greater part of their wages in the city. The Gloster Aircraft Company had decided to move from Sunningend, Cheltenham, to Hucclecote in 1925, but this took several years to accomplish. (James, D., *Gloster Aircraft Company*, 1994)

OCTOBER 6TH

1814: John Pope appeared before the City Magistrates, charged with throwing 'a quantity of filth and rubbish' into the Gloucester & Berkeley Canal, at about half past ten at night on October 1st. (*Calendar of Summary Convictions at Petty Sessions, 1781-1837*, ed. I. Wyatt, Gloucestershire Record Series, Volume 22, 2008)

———◆———

1846: A fire broke out on the premises of the Birmingham and Gloucester Railway Company at Gloucester, between six and seven o'clock in the evening. The city and neighbourhood were illuminated for many miles by the flames. Three fire engines speedily arrived at the scene, as did thousands of spectators. As the fire raged, it became obvious that the engine room could not be saved, but great efforts were made to stop the flames spreading to other buildings. Within an hour, the fire was subdued to a great extent. (*The Citizen*)

OCTOBER 7TH

1948: The annual produce exhibition of the County Federation of Women's Institutes was opened at the Guildhall, by Miss Isla Woodcock of Lypiatt Park, Chairman of the Gloucestershire Women's Institutes' Markets Ltd. There was an impressive display of nearly 400 exhibits, in fifty classes.

Entries in the preserves and bottled fruit and vegetable classes were particularly strong, and some 300 jars of jam, marmalade and jelly kept the judges busy. Additional classes this year included one for household polishes. A demonstration of miniature posies and flower decorations was another new feature. (*Cheltenham Chronicle*)

———◆———

1895: The Second Gloucester Mop was held on this day, and a good number of farmhands were seen standing about the Cross, waiting to be hired. The event prompted an old resident, who only identified himself by the initials 'H.Y.J.T.', to reminisce about the Mop. He remembered as a boy being shocked to see crowds of men and women assembled at the Cross, like cattle and horses, eagerly waiting to be hired. He had been equally shocked to hear the rude and course questions which the women were asked by the hirers. At that time, he said, country women 'were no more respected than beasts of burden'. The practice was 'a degradation to a Christian society' and he hoped the Mop would soon die out altogether. (*The Citizen*)

OCTOBER 8TH

1861: It was reported that Viscount Forth, the only son of the Earl of Perth, had killed himself at the Spa Hotel in Gloucester. Forth, whose full name was the Hon. George Henry Charles Francis Malcolm Drummond, had been embroiled in a divorce suit brought by his wife, because of his infidelity. Lady Forth was having an affair too, and both parties were deemed to be as bad as each other.

Forth and a lady came to Gloucester in July 1861 and they gave their names at the Spa Hotel as Captain and Mrs Drummond. The lady, whose real name was Mrs Lloyd, gave birth to a daughter on September 19th, but the new mother became ill and died on October 8th. Forth was inconsolable and began drinking heavily. Later, a nurse saw him take a swig from a laudanum bottle. He had managed to swallow half of the contents before it was taken off him. He also tried to cut his throat. A doctor was sent for and later his stomach was pumped, but he died. The orphaned daughter of the pair was baptised Ann Cooper Lloyd, but she died soon afterwards, at Longford. Viscount Forth was buried at Gloucester Cemetery. (*The Penny Illustrated*; www.peerage.com)

OCTOBER 9TH

1878: At the Gloucester Petty Sessions, Jane Pritchard, a young woman, was sent to prison for ten days, for using obscene language in Southgate Street. (*The Citizen*)

———•◆•———

1942: The annual autumn show held by Messrs Bruton, Knowles and Co. took place at the Cattle Market. Good quality cattle were exhibited, including Shorthorn, British Fresian, and Guernsey cows, heifers, and pedigree and non-pedigree bulls. Over 100 lots were put up for sale after the show.

The Silver Challenge Cup was presented by Messrs Foster Bros, of the Gloucester branch of the British Oil and Cake Mills Ltd, for the best dairy cow or heifer of any breed. It was won by Messrs F.E. Exell & Son of White House Farm, Cam, with a British Fresian cow with calf, by a Fresian bull. This lot later sold for 100 guineas. Congratulating the winners, Norman Bruton said it was the first time they had gained a success with a Fresian, although they had been successful with Shorthorns. Mr Bruton later said that the show was the best he had held. (*The Citizen*)

OCTOBER 10TH

1891: On this Saturday, Gloucester Rugby Club's new ground opened at Kingsholm. The club had been formed in September 1873, and played its first game on a piece of land in Dean's Walk, where the Kingsholm ground was later built. After that game, the club's home matches were played at the Spa ground. Gloucester held its first gate-taking fixture there on February 12th 1876, against London club, the Flamingoes. The Spa continued as Gloucester's home ground until the move was made to Kingsholm in 1891.

The new ground was built on the Castle Grim estate in Dean's Walk. On its opening day, Gloucester played against Burton. As befitted the occasion, the home team won. (gloucesterrugbyheritage.co.uk; *The Citizen*)

1896: In the early hours of the morning, Gloucester Fire Brigade was called out to Elmbridge Court near Gloucester, to the residence of Melville Harvey, Master of the Longford beagles. A fire had broken out in one of the outbuildings, and was not extinguished until a considerable amount of damage had been done. Two policemen who discovered the fire were able to save some valuable horses from the stables. (*Lloyds Weekly*)

OCTOBER 11TH

1784: A highway robbery was committed at the bottom of Barton Street. Two men jumped out of a lane that went towards Tredworth and attacked Edward Summers, a carpenter, who was returning home to Pitchcombe after the Barton Mop. The men demanded his money or his life. One of the men held Summers' hands behind his back, while the other robbed him of five shillings, some halfpennies and a penknife. The villain opened the knife and swore he would cut Summers' throat if he didn't produce more money. Summers assured him that he had nothing more, and the other robber said, 'Don't hurt him if he has given all his money'. The first man replied, 'Damn me, but I'll ear mark him', and cut off almost all of Summers' left ear.

After the robbery, a search was made in the local taverns, and one David Castell was arrested on suspicion. Summers swore he was the man who held his hands. David Castell was hanged for committing highway robbery in April 1785. (*Hereford Times*)

OCTOBER 12TH

1932: Gloucester City Council made civic history on this day, when at a committee meeting it was decided to ask Mr W.L. Edwards to accept the office of the first Labour Mayor of the city, and also asked Mr Charles Fox to become its first Labour City High Sheriff. Both men had, in the past, unsuccessfully contested Parliamentary elections in Gloucester as Labour Party candidates. Mr Edwards, one of the senior members of the council, who had served for a short time as an alderman, stood for Labour in the 1918 election. Mr Fox was a veteran socialist who had lost to Mr H. Leslie Boyce at the last General Election. Both men were in the dental profession, and both were enthusiastic Dickensians. (*Cheltenham Chronicle*)

———— • ◆ • ————

1886: The following appeared under 'Late Advertisements' in *The Citizen*:

Mrs Hall, Bristol Road, Gloucester.
Madam – We the undersigned, DESIRE TO OFFER YOU A SINCERE APOLOGY for having assaulted you on Saturday, October 9th, 1886. R. Gibson, E. Gibson.
Mrs Hall, Sudbrook Restaurant, Gloucester, October 12th, 1886.

OCTOBER 13TH

1837: The members of the Gloucestershire Yeomanry Cavalry had been gathered together in Gloucester for a week, for their annual session of training and exercise, under the command of Lt-Col the Hon. James Dutton. The regiment mustered at 400-strong, and presented 'a very soldier-like appearance'. The men were formed into four troops: the Doddington and Tetbury; the Badminton and Cirencester; the Gloucester and Stroud; and the Alveston and Winterbourne and Stapleton.

On this final day, the inspection of the corps took place, and an immense number of spectators came to Gloucester to watch, many of whom were 'of the first families of the county'. At midday, the ground filled with 'a numerous and brilliant assemblage of company'. Colonel his Grace the Duke of Beaufort, who had been unable to attend the earlier training and exercises because of a violent attack of gout, was present, but obviously suffering. The manoeuvres were conducted by Lt-Col Dutton, and watched by the Inspecting Field Officer, Colonel Greenwood of the Second Life Guards.

Considering the limited amount of time the troops had for training together, they were surprisingly efficient. On the conclusion of the display, Colonel Greenwood addressed them, congratulating them on their performance and expressing astonishment at the regularity and precision of their movements. He said he would be making a most favourable report on their abilities. (*Bath Chronicle*)

OCTOBER 14TH

1892: A Cyclists' Lantern Parade was held in Gloucester, organised by the Gloucester Cycling Club. Starting in the Old Spa field, the site was transformed by many oriental lanterns attached to bicycles and tricycles of all shapes and sizes, from the latest pneumatic models to the original old 'bone-shakers'. Shortly after half past eight in the evening, buglers from the Gloucester Artillery, the Dock Rifles and the City Rifles sounded, and the procession of nearly 200 cyclists set off, headed by the band of the Royal Gloucester Engineers.

The long line made its way along Spa Road, to Southgate Street, Northgate Street, Wotton, Denmark Road, Priory Road, Westgate Street, Eastgate Street, Parkend Road, Stroud Road, Bristol Road, and back to the Spa ground. Gloucester Cycling Club members led the way, followed by cycling clubs Atlas, Barnwood, Southgate, Gloucester Conservative Club, Tynedale, City Steam Press and Liberal, and lastly riders of no particular club. It took twenty minutes for the procession to pass any particular spot.

There were quite a few accidents, mostly because of earlier rain, which had made the roads slippery, although some were caused by spectators getting in the way. The whole parade took about one and a half hours to complete. It was followed by a smoking concert at the Liberal Club. (*The Citizen*)

OCTOBER 15TH

1783: Thomas Rudhall, of the famous Gloucester bell-founding family, died. He was the great-grandson of the man who, in 1684, started up the business, Abraham Rudhall. The bell-foundry passed down the male line to Abraham Rudhall junior and then to Abel Rudhall. When Abel died, the business was left to his three sons from his first marriage – Abraham, Thomas and Charles, who were all in their teens. Thomas ran the business with the help of the bell-foundry manager, Francis Tyler. It was this Thomas Rudhall who died in 1783.

Thomas bequeathed his share in the business to his brothers, Abraham and Charles, but Abraham relinquished his part to his half-brother John, in return for a payment. Charles and John continued as partners until Charles retired in 1787. John then continued on his own until 1829, when the business was sold to the Whitechapel Bell Foundry. The bells made in Gloucester continued to bear the name of John Rudhall until he died. Between 1684 and 1835, it was estimated that the Rudhall bell foundry produced over 5,000 bells. (*Gloucester Journal*; Bliss, M., 'The Last Years of John Rudhall, Bellfounder of Gloucester', in *Transactions of the Bristol and Gloucestershire Archaeological Society*, Volume 121)

OCTOBER 16TH

1911: Bentfield Charles Hucks, one of the early aviators, came to Gloucester to give an exhibition of flying. At Port Ham, he thrilled spectators by flying his Blackburn Monoplane to a height of 1,000 feet. Back on the ground, he was given a civic reception by the Mayor, the Corporation, and members of the Council.

Hucks had been a motor-racing driver, but had his driving licence suspended for three years after being convicted of speeding, so he had turned his attention to aeroplanes. He started flying in 1910, and got his Royal Aero Club certificate in May 1911. The visit to Gloucester was part of a tour of the West of England, and he had performed at Cheltenham the week before.

At the outbreak of war in 1914, he volunteered for active service and was sent to France, but he contracted pleurisy and was unable to continue. He became a test pilot for new aeroplanes, attached to the Aircraft Manufacturing Company. On November 7th 1918, Hucks died at the age of 35, having contracted Spanish Influenza. (*Cheltenham Looker-on*; http://earlyaviators.com)

OCTOBER 17TH

1864: The funeral took place of Sergeant Major Henry Allen, of the Gloucester Militia and Dock Rifle Company. He had killed himself with a rifle on October 11th. Allen had been highly esteemed by his fellow non-commissioned officers and by the Volunteers. He had been the drill instructor to the Dock Rifle Company from its formation about five years previously, and had charge of the Militia Armoury, where he lived with his wife and six children.

Despite his popularity, there had been a disagreement between him and a Sergeant Holyoake, who had accused him of some dishonesty involving money, which seemed to prey on his mind. On the morning of October 11th, he got up and had breakfast, then went into the guard room and blew his brains out with a rifle, using his foot to set off the trigger.

At the funeral, the Militia, Artillery and Rifle bands joined in playing the *Dead March*. A subscription was opened for his widow and children. Sergeant Holyoake was dismissed from the regiment for insubordination and using disrespectful language. (*Western Daily Press*)

OCTOBER 18TH

1878: At about a quarter past six in the evening, the Fire Office received reports that a fire had been discovered at Gloucester Wagon Works, which was spreading rapidly. The joinery department of the Works was on fire and a large saw mill was in flames. The Works abutted the canal, and water from it was used to try to douse the flames, but just as the spray hit, there was a loud explosion, believed to be caused by the fire igniting the building's gas supply. The fire caught hold of adjoining buildings and spread rapidly. The sheds were carpenters' shops, all built of wood.

An east wind kept the fire from the main portion of the Works, but there were fears that it would spread to the adjoining timber yards of Messrs Price and Co. About an hour after its discovery, the fire began to abate. All the buildings in a square of about 70 to 100 yards were destroyed. It was believed that the fire had begun beneath the floor in an apartment adjoining the engine room. The workers had tried to put it out with their own extinguishing equipment, before calling the Fire Brigade. (*Gloucester Journal*)

OCTOBER 19TH

1905: The New Zealand rugby team played a match against Gloucester at Kingsholm, watched by around 14,000 spectators. The day was treated as a holiday in the city.

Gloucester held up well against the visitors until one of their players, Hudson, was badly stunned and had to leave the field. Gloucester were severely handicapped and New Zealand scored with such rapidity that before the interval came, they had scored 26 points. After the interval, Hudson came back on and Gloucester recovered – it was thirty minutes before New Zealand scored again. Then Gloucester's half back, Wood, twisted his ankle and had to be carried off the field. The end result was a win for New Zealand by 44 points to nil. (*The Citizen*)

———◆———

1830: The Duchess of Kent and her daughter, Princess Victoria (later Queen Victoria), came to Gloucester. They visited all the attractions of the city and were highly delighted with their reception by the good people of Gloucester. (*Bath Chronicle*)

OCTOBER 20TH

1927: The 7th Gloucester (Good Templar) Troop of Scouts opened their new headquarters at the rear of the Institute of Good Templars Hall, Suffolk House, Greyfriars. Mr Matthews, as chairman of the committee responsible for the management of the hall, gave a hearty welcome to the scouts in their new home. (*Gloucester Journal*)

1956: It was reported in the local press that the Roberts Brothers' toy factory in Gloucester was to be closed down and the business moved to Birmingham. The 198 workers were told that if they had worked for the company for ten years or more they would be offered posts with other factories belonging to the parent company, Chad Valley. This applied to thirty-three employees. The others were given three months' notice, and interviews were organised with the employment services.

Roberts Brothers, manufacturers of card and wooden games, had been founded in about 1888 by Alderman John Roberts, who was Mayor of Gloucester five times and City High Sheriff six times, and his brother Harry Roberts. As the business developed, it moved to Llanthony Road, and then in 1902 moved into the Glevum Works. (*The Citizen*)

OCTOBER 21ST

1914: With the outbreak of war, the Red Cross began to set up Voluntary Aid (VA) hospitals to supplement the existing military and civilian hospitals. The VA hospitals were run by Voluntary Aid Detachments, who were usually unpaid local women. They were initially set up to care for Belgian soldiers sent to Britain for treatment, but soon became flooded with British casualties. In Gloucester, a VA hospital was opened on this day, on the site of the partially completed new infirmary building at the Gloucester Union Workhouse. By 1916, more beds were needed, and a committee of Gloucester citizens provided a hut, complete with electric light, baths, sanitary accommodation and a dining room, which was built and occupied within seventeen days. This meant the hospital had 272 beds and, with an annex at Boddington raising that number to 290, it was one of the largest VA hospitals in the country. In the four and a half years between its opening and March 20th 1919, the hospital admitted 4,822 patients, of whom thirty-one died. (*The Red Cross in Gloucestershire, 1914-19*, on www. angelfire.com)

OCTOBER 22ND

1378: King Richard II held parliament at Gloucester from this day until November 16th. It was the second year of his reign, and he was just 11 years old. The visit caused a great deal of disruption and inconvenience in the Abbey and the town. The King lodged at the Abbey, bringing his whole family and retinue with him. The Abbey was so full with the royal party and members of parliament that on some days the monks had to eat in the dormitory or the school, and meals were prepared in the orchard. The green of the cloister was flattened by ball games and wrestling, which damaged the grass.

The business of parliament was carried out in the Abbey, with the Council of the Commons meeting in the Chapter House, and the Lords in the Great Hall. (Wallander, D., *The History, Art and Architecture of Gloucester Cathedral*, 1991)

OCTOBER 23RD

2009: Queen Elizabeth II, accompanied by the Duke of Edinburgh, visited Gloucester Docks, to see the recent development and regeneration which had been taking place there. The royal couple arrived in Gloucester by helicopter, then boarded a boat which came up the canal and into the basin. Disembarking at the Quayside, they were met by the Lord Lieutenant of Gloucestershire, Henry Elwes, and the party made its way past the ruins of Llanthony Secunda Priory to Gloucestershire College.

In Gloucester, hundreds of people gathered to see the royal party, waving flags which had been given out by the City Council. Brownies, cadets, police officers and others lined the Queen's path as she made her way from the Docks to the college. Inside the college building, the Lord Lieutenant introduced the Queen to Mr Mohamed Patel, the chairman of Barton and Tredworth Trust Volunteers. She also met members of the Gloucester regeneration team and developers. The party then made its way to the dining room for lunch, which had been prepared by the staff and the top thirty students of the college's catering academy.

After lunch, the Queen and the Duke of Edinburgh were invited to sign the college's visitor book, before they left Gloucester and paid a visit to GCHQ in Cheltenham. (*The Citizen*)

OCTOBER 24TH

1878: New schools at Widden Street were opened by the Gloucester School Board. The schools consisted of a boys' school in one block, and a girls' and infants' school in another. The establishment could accommodate up to 600 children, although it wasn't expected that there would be this number for some time.

The opening ceremony took place in the girls' schoolroom. The Chairman (Revd Nisbet) said that they were there to open the first school built by the Gloucester School Board. The Board had been established to meet a deficiency of school places, and the law had given them the power of compelling parents to send their children between the ages of 5 and 13 years to school. (*The Citizen*)

———◆•◆———

1757: Button Gwinnett, son of Samuel Gwinnett, clerk, was registered as a Freeman of Gloucester. Born in Down Hatherley, Gwinnett was baptised at St Catherine's parish church in Gloucester and went to the King's School. He later moved to Wolverhampton, and in 1762 he emigrated to America. He became a successful plantation owner in Georgia, and was elected to the Provincial Assembly in 1769. In 1776, he signed his name to the Declaration of Independence. (*A Calendar of the Registers of Freemen of the City of Gloucester, 1641-1838*, ed. J. Jurica, Gloucestershire Record Series, Volume 4, 1991; *Encyclopedia Britannica*)

OCTOBER 25TH

1906: Great excitement was caused in Gloucester by the break-out of some convicts from the County Prison. The ringleader was Michel Harnett, alias 'London Mike', who, with the help of a second prisoner, overpowered two warders, stole their keys and locked them in the cells. They released three other prisoners and overpowered the sentry on the gate. They then commandeered a boat and forced its owner to row them to the other side of the river. One of the men soon tired of the adventure and gave himself up at a railway signal box, where the signalman alerted the police. The other men made their way into the Forest of Dean.

At four o'clock the next morning, a policeman in Westbury-on-Severn spotted the four in their conspicuous arrow-patterned uniforms and followed them. They were eventually captured the following afternoon, and were so tired that they didn't put up any fight. They were brought back from Lydney to Gloucester by train. It was said that as London Mike passed back through the prison gates in a wagon, he waved his hand and shouted, 'Say *au revoir*, but not goodbye'. (*The Citizen*)

OCTOBER 26TH

1889: Gloucester City Association Football Club, founded in 1883, played its first competitive game at Budding's Field. In the first round of the Gloucestershire FA Junior Challenge Cup, the home team beat Clifton Association Reserves by ten goals to nil.

In 1934, Gloucester turned semi-professional and moved to a new ground at Longlevens, where they stayed for twenty-six years. In 1964, another move was made, to the Horton Road stadium. In 1986, Gloucester moved to Meadow Park. This ground was prone to occasional flooding, and the club was badly hit by serious floods in 1990 and 2000. The worst incident came in July 2007, with the terrible flooding that engulfed all of Gloucester. At Meadow Park, the water was 8 feet deep. In the following season, Gloucester City played its home games at Forest Green Rovers' ground. In the 2008/9 season, the club played at Cirencester Town's ground, and from the 2010/11 season, the club shared Cheltenham's ground. (www. gloucestercityafc.com)

OCTOBER 27TH

1924: An unusual trial began at the Gloucester City Assizes, when local doctor Walter Robert Hadwen, a well-known campaigner against vaccination for smallpox, was charged with manslaughter by giving improper medical treatment to a child, who died. The illness which killed 10-year-old Nellie Christobelle Burnham was not smallpox, but diphtheria, followed by pneumonia. The prosecution's case was that Dr Hadwen had failed to diagnose diphtheria and had not visited the girl as often as he should have. It came out in court, though, that the child's mother had not told the doctor when her daughter's condition grew much worse, saying she had expected him to visit anyway, without being summoned. Nellie's uncle had called in his own doctor, Dr Ellis, who happened to be an old enemy of Hadwen's.

When Hadwen gave his evidence, he told the judge that he was an anti-vivisectionist, so he did not approve of vaccinations or toxins being used in treatment, because they had been tested on animals. He also maintained that the treatments did not work and could cause more harm than they did good. Two days after the trial began, Hadwen was found not guilty. The verdict was greeted by cheers from his supporters in the courtroom, and among the crowds in the streets. (*The Citizen*)

OCTOBER 28TH

1216: Henry III was crowned at Gloucester Cathedral (then St Peter's Abbey). Born on October 1st 1207, Henry was the son of King John and Queen Isabel. He became King of England on October 19th 1216, when he was just 9 years old. Queen Isabel was keen to have her son crowned as soon as possible, because Louis, the King of France, controlled all of eastern England, including London, and was recognised as King of England by the majority of the English barons.

Contemporary chronicles said that Henry was carried into the Cathedral, dressed in royal robes made to his size. He was crowned by the legate Gualo, representing Pope Honorius III, assisted by the Bishops assembled there. Henry had a second coronation in Westminster Cathedral three years later. William Marshall, Earl of Pembroke, became Regent while Henry was a minor, and within a year had defeated Louis. In 1227, Henry became king in his own right, and reigned for fifty-six years. (*Chronicles of the Age of Chivalry*, ed. E. Hallam, 1987)

OCTOBER 29TH

1588: Richard Pate is usually associated with Cheltenham, because he founded Pate's Grammar School in the town, but he had a long association with Gloucester, where he was the Recorder from 1561 until his death on this day. Pate was the nephew of another Richard Pate, who was Bishop of Worcester until 1559. His place of birth is not known for certain, but was probably Cheltenham. Later, he lived in Gloucester, and also had a house in Minsterworth. He trained as a lawyer and represented Gloucester in Parliament several times. As Recorder, he took part in many of the significant decisions and events in Gloucester in the third quarter of the sixteenth century. Because of his importance in the town and borough, he was buried in Gloucester Cathedral. (*Oxford Dictionary of National Biography*)

———◆———

1881: A notice in *The Graphic* stated that the question now being asked by everyone was how this coming 'winter of discontent' could be 'made like glorious summer' by a well-warmed house. Those who wanted to learn how this could be achieved cheaply, healthily and effectively by the new EUTHERMIC appliances (Dr Bond's Patents; awarded two medals by the Sanitary Institute of Great Britain) should write to the Sanitary and Oeconomic Supply Association Ltd, Gloucester. (*The Graphic*)

OCTOBER 30TH

1935: A debate was held by Gloucester City Council concerning new swimming baths which were planned for Gloucester. The question was whether to have an open-air swimming pool or a covered-over baths. The Baths Committee recommended the covered-over option, but Mrs M.I. Edwards moved an amendment that the facilities should be open air. She pointed out that Cheltenham had an open air-bath, which had proved a great success during the last summer season. Councillor Tyte pointed out that Cheltenham's success had been due to the fact that the country had recently enjoyed a cycle of fine summers. Unless the English climate changed, we could expect a cycle of bad ones in the near future. The council decided on a covered-over bath, Mrs Edwards' amendment being defeated by twenty-one votes to eleven. (*Bath Chronicle*)

1858: The last remaining prisoner at the City Gaol in Southgate Street, a debtor, was released, and the establishment was closed down. It had been decided that there were not enough city prisoners to justify keeping the building open. In future, city prisoners would be sent to the County Prison. (*Western Daily Press*)

OCTOBER 31ST

1906: At Gloucester City Petty Sessions, George Hurd, a shopkeeper at No. 70 High Street, Tredworth, appeared, charged with selling explosives to a child apparently under the age of 13 years, on October 19th, and with selling fireworks on unregistered premises on the same date.

The defendant pleaded guilty, but under ignorance, to the first charge. He was not aware that he was doing anything wrong. PC Lane said he had observed a 7-year-old girl purchasing a halfpenny's worth of Chinese Crackers. With regard to the second charge, Deputy Chief Constable Harrison said the defendant was a respectable man, who appeared to be a cripple, and he did not wish to press the case. He only wanted it to be made known that people must not sell fireworks to children under 13 years of age, and they must not store them on unregistered premises. The Chairman said no doubt the Press would call attention to this. The defendant was let off with payment of the expenses. (*The Citizen*)

NOVEMBER 1ST

1733: In the early hours of the morning, the Over turnpike, near Gloucester, was attacked by a group of people armed with guns, pistols and axes. People living in the neighbourhood were threatened with death if they looked at the gang from out of their windows. A few weeks later, a notice was published in the press, promising a pardon from King George II to any of the gang who gave up his accomplices. A reward of £50 was also offered to anyone who had significant information, which would be paid upon the conviction of the offenders. (*The London Gazette*)

———◆———

1893: Municipal elections took place on a bitterly cold day. It wasn't clear on the day which party, if any, had a majority, but on the next day it was announced that the Conservatives had returned eight out of nine of their candidates, and had gained four seats. This meant the comfortable majority in the council, which the Liberals had enjoyed for years, was replaced by a balance of power between the Conservatives and the Liberals. (*The Citizen*)

NOVEMBER 2ND

1902: A letter was printed in *The Citizen* concerning the Council's decision to erect a public convenience for ladies on a site in Bell Lane, where a house was to be demolished to make way for the new building. The decision had prompted many protests at the £2,750 cost of the accepted tender.

The letter, from 'A Ratepayer', wanted to know why the old Weights and Measures office in Brunswick Road, which was close to falling down, had not been chosen as the site, as it was in an ideal spot and not surrounded by public houses.

The Council had actually been trying for some time to find somewhere for the 'public sanitary conveniences for females', but the various sites had always been objected to. In May, the Gloucester Streets Committee had recommended that the Council approve the site in Bell Lane. The issue had been debated at length, the main objection to the scheme being the estimated cost, although some disapproved of the position, near to various public houses. It was clear that there was a need for more ladies' toilets, because for the eight months that a temporary facility in Berkeley Street had been open, 20,000 pennies had been collected. (*The Citizen*)

November 3rd

1906: Kingsholm rugby football ground hosted a game between Gloucestershire and the South Africans, who were in the country on tour, prior to playing international games against England, Scotland, Ireland and Wales. The Springboks had already played eleven matches against other county teams, and had won all of them. It was hoped that the Gloucestershire team, which contained four international players, would give the visitors more of a match. The county side was made up of six Gloucester players, four from Bristol, two from Cinderford, one each from Lydney and Cheltenham, plus one player from Devon Albion.

At Kingsholm, accommodation had been provided for up to 14,000 spectators, with an extra stand being put up in the ground. The stands were full by the time the teams ran out onto the field. Both sides were greeted by hearty cheers. Despite the presence of players of international standard in the home side, they were beaten by the Springboks, the final score being 23 points to nil. (*The Citizen*)

NOVEMBER 4TH

1840: The Birmingham and Gloucester Railway began running trains between Gloucester and Cheltenham on this day. The opening day was intended to be November 2nd, but an inspection had found that work was not quite complete. The inspector was given assurances that two lines of rails would be laid before opening and this, together with repairs to a defective bridge at Barnwood, delayed the opening.

The Birmingham and Gloucester Railway Company had been authorised to build a line by Act of Parliament in 1836. The first stretch had opened between Bromsgrove and Cheltenham, in June 1840. Experimental runs on the new section between Cheltenham and Gloucester had been made on October 17th, when passengers had been allowed free trips between the two stations. The official opening took place on a cold, wet morning. The inaugural journey from Landsdown Road to Gloucester took sixteen minutes, and the train arrived to be greeted by crowds of people. (Long, P.J., and Awdry, Revd W.V.A., *The Birmingham and Gloucester Railway*, 1987)

———— ◆ ————

1962: Larry Parnes brought his 'Mammoth Star Show of 1962' to the Regal in Gloucester, for one night only. The headline acts were Billy Fury and Marty Wilde, and also on the bill were the Karl Denver Trio, Joe Brown and the Bruvvers, Mike Sarne, Mark Wynter, Jimmy Justice, and Peter Jay and the Jaywalkers. (bradfordtimeline.co.uk)

NOVEMBER 5TH

1883: The people of Longlevens celebrated Bonfire Night with a public show of disapproval against a miscreant living in their midst. It appeared that amongst its inhabitants lived a wife-beater. An effigy of this man replaced the usual representation of Guy Fawkes, which was hung by the neck for a considerable length of time, before being set alight, watched by hundreds of spectators. (*The Citizen*)

———— • ◆ • ————

1836: In the *Gloucester Journal* of this day, it was reported that following an incident in which a little boy got wedged inside a chimney for thirteen hours, after he had been sent up to sweep it, some citizens, who had a machine that cleaned chimneys, had found a man who was willing to take on the job of operating it. People who used boys as chimney sweeps always argued that 'Mr Glass's machine' did not do as good a job. Several prominent citizens had tried out the machine and reported that it worked very efficiently if it was operated correctly. Some said it was so clean that even ladies could remain in the room during the process. (*Gloucester Journal*)

NOVEMBER 6TH

1788: Following the discovery of a spring in Westgate Street, a spa pump room was opened on this date. The spring had been found on ground behind Eagle House, belonging to the Duke of Norfolk. The spa was popular for a while, but public enthusiasm quickly faded, with Cheltenham being so close by.

In 1814, another spring was discovered on land belonging to Sir James Jelf. A pump room was built and opened in 1815. The houses in Spa Road were built after the opening. Although it did better than the Westgate Street spa, competition with the more fashionable Cheltenham again meant that the venture didn't last. The Corporation bought the grounds in 1861 and opened the public park there. The springs closed in 1894 and the Pump Room was demolished in 1960. (*Gloucester Journal*; Kirby, D., *The Story of Gloucester*, 2007)

NOVEMBER 7TH

1939: Queen Mary made an informal visit to Gloucestershire Training College in Gloucester. Because of wartime security, few people had been made aware of her visit. She saw some of the work in progress at the college and took tea with the principal (Miss R. Whittaker) and the Chairman of the Governing Body (Sir Ronald Kerr) at the Bishop's Palace. She accepted a book on communal dietaries in wartime, recently published by the college.

The Bishop's Palace had been lent by the Bishop for accommodation for some of the students, because the college hall of residence had been commandeered. Before coming to Gloucester, Queen Mary had made a visit to Huntley. (*Gloucester Journal*)

NOVEMBER 8TH

1884: A collision took place in the evening between two carts. A milk cart, owned by Mr Portman of Bristol Road, was standing close to the pavement opposite the residence of Mr Hastie in Howard Street. Miss Portman, who was delivering the milk, had just seated herself and was preparing to drive towards Conduit Street, when another cart collided with hers from behind, throwing her out and causing her head to strike the pavement so violently that she was insensible for some time and had to be driven home. A large can of milk was upset in the street. It was said that the driver of the second cart drove on, leaving the unfortunate woman to be cared for by passers-by. (*The Citizen*)

NOVEMBER 9TH

1891: At a Town Council meeting held on this morning, the election of the Mayor, Sheriff and other officials took place, with a large attendance of councillors and also of the general public. The Mayor appeared in the ancient garment known as 'Dame Cooke's cloak'. He said he was wearing it in accordance with ancient custom, and to keep the memory of Dame Joan (the founder of the Crypt School) alive. She had left the cloak to the city, and it was nearly 400 years old.

Alderman Platt (of Fielding and Platt) was elected to be the new Mayor. The retiring mayor, Mr Seekings, robed him in Dame Joan's cloak and placed the chain of office around his neck. Alderman Platt was not a native of the city, but had lived in Gloucester for over thirty years, and was one of the biggest employers in the area.

Mr J.B. Karn was elected Sheriff and Mr H. Mousel was announced as the Deputy Mayor. Mr Read was re-elected as City Chamberlain at a salary of £300, Mr Matthews as sword-bearer, at £5, Mr Miles Brook as Town Crier and Mr W.J. Davis as Freeman's Hayward; the Mayor's salary remained fixed at £240. (*The Citizen*)

NOVEMBER 10TH

1888: At the County Petty Sessions, Sydney Gwilliam was charged with killing a racing pigeon belonging to Arthur Smith, a member of the Gloucester Glevum Homing Club. Smith had let the pigeon out for exercise and saw the defendant shoot it from an adjoining field. The prosecution was brought by the Homing Club, which wanted to make it known that people shouldn't kill racing pigeons because they were quite valuable when alive, but were worth next to nothing when dead. The defendant was fined 1 shilling and ordered to pay £1 in damages. (*The Citizen*)

———◆———

1900: The following was published in *The Citizen*:

APOLOGY

To Mrs. ROSE HARRIET KING, of No. 12, Stratton Rd, City of Glo.

I FANNIE CRITCHLEY, of No. 6, Hopewell Street, Glo., hereby apologise to you for the abusive and unjustifiable language which I made use of to you and respecting you for which I admit there was no foundation whatsoever, and I express my sincere regret for the annoyance I have thus caused you and undertake not to repeat the same.

Dated this 8th day of November, 1900.

FANNIE CRITCHLEY.

(Witness) Thomas Bent Phillips, Clerk to Mr. W. Langley-Smith, Solicitor, Gloucester.

NOVEMBER 11TH

1895: A team of lady footballers played a match at Kingsholm. The reporter sent to watch the evening game was not impressed. 'The weather was awful, the pitch was muddy and the ball was greasy. The players betrayed an anxiety natural to their sex to avoid hurting one another, and a disinclination to fall in the mud. Their costume did not help freedom of movement, consisting of a blouse and bloomers, which were modest and would have been picturesque if they hadn't been stained and weather-beaten.' There were a couple of players who showed some talent. A lady called 'Tommy' was really clever with some dribbles and was much faster and more agile than some of her team-mates. The goalkeepers were men, who weren't so gallant as to allow the ladies of the opposite team to get a ball into the net, so there were no goals. Fifteen minutes into the second half, it rained so hard that the game was stopped. The spectators had come to scoff, and did so, but there was a big crowd, and £55 was taken on the gate. (*The Citizen*)

NOVEMBER 12TH

1926: The weekly luncheon of the Gloucester Rotary Club was held at the Spread Eagle Hotel. President J.A.J. Venmore was the Chair and introduced Mr F. Madison, who gave a talk on 'Rotarian Ideals and International Peace'. Mr Madison said that Rotary existed for the advancement of understanding, good-will and international peace, through a world fellowship of business and professional men, united in the Rotary ideal of service. He argued that it was possible to love one's own country and still be an 'internationalist'. Some people seemed to think that Providence made a mistake when anyone else was created but Englishmen – and perhaps Scotsmen (laughter). But the world would be a miserable place if one saw nothing but the English type. Rotarians could not think anymore of foreigners as enemies; rather they should be looked on as neighbours. The speaker was heartily thanked for his address. (*The Citizen*)

NOVEMBER 13TH

1962: The world-famous percussionist James Blades lectured and entertained children from all the Gloucester junior schools at the Guildhall. The children sat almost without fidgeting as Mr Blades, accompanied by pianist Miss Joan Goossens, demonstrated the various blocks, bells, cymbals, tambourines and gongs which make up the percussion section of an orchestra. He explained the history of the instruments as well as their place in the orchestra, and children were invited on stage to try them out.

The highlight of the afternoon was a Chinese gong on which Mr Blades did a lifelike impression of a jet plane, causing the building to shake and forcing the audience to put their fingers in their ears. Also, to show he was no 'square', he confided that he liked just a little rock n' roll, and did a drum solo which equalled the best from the Top Twenty. (*The Citizen*)

NOVEMBER 14TH

1885: At the County Petty Sessions, six boys of various ages answered to their names. Mr Golding, of Hempsted, said that on the previous Sunday, the boys were driving his horses round the field, trying to make them jump the fences. He caught the oldest boy, who gave several wrong names. No fences were damaged and none of the horses were harmed, but it was a nuisance that he wished to put a stop to, and they had been warned to appear so that they might be reprimanded.

The Chairman (Sir W.V. Guise) told the boys he could not see what pleasure they would derive from doing mischief. It must be a spirit of devilry in them, for nobody with an ounce of brains would do such a thing. They were then discharged.

Next up were some more mischievous boys, namely Albert Blake, aged 14, Reece Payne, 12, Sidney Hughes, 14, and Robert Hughes, 10, who were summonsed for breaking down a hedge, the property of Mr T. Barnard of Tuffley. Mr Barnard said the boys caused 6 pence worth of damage to the hedge when they tried to climb over it. The boys were discharged on their parents paying the costs of the prosecution. (*The Citizen*)

November 15th

1799: It was announced in the local press that on this night, Signor Rossignol would give a performance of his imitations of birds, in the Council Chamber at the Booth Hall. (*Gloucester Journal*)

———— ••• ————

1906: Gloucester suffered a powercut, when the electricity supply had a temporary failure, caused by the heating of a bearing in one of the engines. The cut interrupted the 'Sunday School eisteddfod', taking place in Shire Hall, which was plunged into darkness. The Chairman of the Electricity Committee, Alderman James Fielding, was in the audience.

The interruption came at an awkward time at the Palace Theatre, where Taro Myaki's show and the cinematograph were delayed for some time. However, the Poole's had gas as a standby, and the show was soon resumed. Taro Myaki, billed as 'Japan's Greatest Wrestler', was the world champion Japanese wrestler, the Mikado's champion and the finest living exponent of the art of Jiu-jitsu. (*The Citizen*)

November 16th

1890: Mrs Elizabeth Fletcher, widow of the late Thomas Fletcher, died at No. 158 Westgate Street. She was said to be a descendant of Shakespeare's sister, Joan, who married a man named Hart. After the second generation of their descendants, the Hart family's property was scattered and mostly went out of the family. Mrs Fletcher owned a cream-coloured earthenware jug and a cane, which were supposed to have belonged to Shakespeare. She hadn't inherited them, however, but had bought them both at sales. The jug had belonged to the Hart family of Tewkesbury.

Mrs Fletcher was the daughter of Richard and Jane Compton and had married Thomas Fletcher, a gun-maker of Tewkesbury, in 1819. She had been in business as a gunsmith for sixty-one years, first with her husband, then for another thirty-two years as a widow. Exactly how she was related to the Hart family was not specified. (*The Citizen*)

November 17th

1868: Parliamentary elections took place at Gloucester on this day, and the excitement in the city was intense. The candidates were the late members, Mr Price and Mr Monk for the Liberals (who had been the subjects of the bribery inquiry in 1859), and Major Lees and Mr Brennan for the Conservatives.

In the afternoon, the shops closed and the streets were thronged with mobs, shouting and indulging in rough play, but overall good-humoured. About 1,000 people hadn't yet voted, and it was thought that they were probably waiting to receive 'an inducement'. Bills had been issued calling attention to the penalties for bribery, and warning that a strict watch would be kept and persons detected would be prosecuted.

The results would not be given until the next day, but it was already obvious that the Liberals would win. The successful candidates thanked their supporters from the windows of the King's Head, while their defeated opponents addressed theirs from the windows of the Bell Hotel. (*Western Daily Press*)

NOVEMBER 18TH

1878: At Gloucester City Police Court, Joseph Emery, an old man, appeared, charged with being drunk and committing a nuisance in the porch of St Nicholas Church in Westgate Street. He was fined 2s 6d, plus 4s 6d costs. If he could not or would not pay, he would spend five days in prison. (*The Citizen*)

———— •✦• ————

1901: At St James's Working Mens' Club, the first 'Ladies Night' of the season took place, and the large club room was filled with members and their lady friends. The usual club games were played for the first hour, then followed a programme of music, consisting of songs, duets (vocal and mandolin), piano solos and recitation. Four men and seven women were the performers. The President, Revd F. Billett, proposed a vote of thanks to the performers, which was heartily carried. The rest of the evening was spent playing parlour games. (*The Citizen*)

———— •✦• ————

1770: Gloucester and the surrounding area was hit by a terrible flood. The part of the city which was nearest the river was under so much water that some inhabitants had to leave their houses, and others were confined to upstairs rooms. In between the Foreign Bridge and the Westgate, there was over 3 feet of water, and boats were used in St Mary's Square, and even in the College churchyard. (*Gloucester Journal*)

November 19th

1900: At Gloucester Police Court, Messrs John Stephens, Son and Co., jam and pickle manufacturers, were summonsed under the Public Health Act, in respect of a nuisance occasioned by their factory chimney at times emitting large quantities of black smoke. The Sanitary Authority had been receiving complaints about the chimney for some time. A notice had been served on them in August 1899, and subsequent notices had been served since, but despite promises made, nothing had been done. The Sanitary Authority said it fully recognised the important industry in which the company were engaged and that recently they had had more work than expected, and were working under pressure. They had now given assurances that they would, without delay, carry out work to abate the nuisance.

Representatives of the company said they were very sorry for the nuisance they had caused over the last year. They had received a very large order from the War Office for their goods to be sent out to the troops in South Africa, and had been too busy to do anything about the chimney. An order was made to abate the nuisance within four months. (*The Citizen*)

NOVEMBER 20TH

1865: The *Western Daily Press* bemoaned the disappearance of one of the most beautiful relics of old Gloucester, which was being pulled down to make room for a new house with a brick front and stone dressings. The Ram Inn had been one of the ancient pilgrim inns in Gloucester, standing in Northgate Street, near St Aldate Street. Three hundred and fifty years ago, the house had been restored by John Osborne, cellarer at the monastery during the time of the last abbot, John Parker. All that remained of the old inn was a beautiful Tudor doorway, elaborately carved with oak leaves and Tudor roses, and bearing a Latin inscription recording that the house had been repaired by John Osborne, 'the town monk'. The old doorway had been admired by every tourist, but was now being removed in preparation for the erection of a shop. The paper hoped the old doorway would be lodged in the museum. (*Western Daily Press*)

NOVEMBER 21ST

1946: The Gloucestershire Regiment was given the Freedom of the City of Gloucester. This gave them the right to march through Gloucester on ceremonial occasions, with colours flying, drums beating and bayonets fixed. Over 100 former officers and their wives, plus about eighty men from other ranks, also with their wives, saw the present representatives of the regiment, 200 officers and men of the 2nd Battalion, exercise the right which had just been conferred upon them.

Brigadier General A.W. Pagan DSO, Colonel of the regiment, received an illuminated address on which was recorded the honour given, from the hands of the Mayor. A message was read out from the Duke of Gloucester, the Colonel-in-Chief, who was in Australia. The reception party had gathered under an awning in front of the Technical College in Brunswick Road, down which the troops marched. After the presentation of the address, the Brigadier General and the Mayor inspected the troops. (*Gloucester Journal*)

NOVEMBER 22ND

1779: Charles Howard, Earl of Surrey, was sworn in as a Freeman of Gloucester. Howard, who later became the Duke of Norfolk, was born in 1746. He married twice, his second wife being Frances Scudamore, through whom he inherited Holme Lacey in Herefordshire, and gained other interests in the Gloucester area. He went on to become an alderman, and was Mayor of Gloucester four times, exerting much political influence in the city. He died in London in 1815, during his final term as Mayor of Gloucester. (*A Calendar of the Registers of the Freemen of the City of Gloucester, 1641-1838*, ed. J. Jurica, Gloucestershire Record Series, Volume 4, 1991; *Morning Post*)

———◆———

1887: The band of the Gloucestershire Engineers were entertained to a supper at the Greyhound Hotel. Over thirty men sat down to a fine meal, under the presidency of George Peters. The cost of the supper was defrayed by the inhabitants of Brunswick Square, on the lawn of which the band had occasionally played during the summer. After supper, a short toast list was gone through. The Chairman proposed 'The band and the officers of the corps', and spoke of the pleasure which their music had given to the Brunswick Square residents. He hoped the band would play there again next year. (*The Citizen*)

NOVEMBER 23RD

1918: During the last year of the Great War, concrete barges were manufactured, in order to save steel supplies. The Gloucester Ferro-Concrete Ship-Building Company Limited, sited at a yard just south of Hempsted graving dock, built six of these concrete barges, and the first was launched on this day. It was named *Creterock*, and was launched before a large company of spectators, including representatives of the British and Italian Admiralties. The others were called *Creteriver*, *Creteroad*, *Creteridge*, *Creteravine*, and *Creterampart*. (Voyce, J., *The City of Gloucester*, 1995; *North Devon Journal*)

1901: The following job advertisements appeared in the 'Situations Vacant' column of *The Citizen*:

- Wanted, Girl (outdoor), just leaving school preferred, for Shop Assistant, must be trustworthy, quick, of respectable parentage. Write stating wages required to 251, Citizen.
- Wanted, Boy, about 15, for pony, boots, etc; might live in house – Address Vicar, Hucclecote.
- Smart Boy wanted for Errands. Mr. Brooke, Bookseller and Stationer, Westgate.
- Sharp Young Lady to learn Fancy Stationery and Leather Goods business – 198, Citizen.
- Wanted, a steady, industrious Young Man (18) to assist with Buns and Pastry. – Apply Roan, Confectioner, Southgate St.

NOVEMBER 24TH

1899: A property sale was held on this day at the New Inn Hotel, conducted by Messrs Bruton, Knowles & Co., at which the total amount realised was £2,240. Annandale House in Barton Street, which had a two-stall stable, a coach-house and a walled garden, and was occupied by Dr Bibby on a lease expiring December 25th 1912, fetched £1,500. The buyer was George Underwood. Four cottages at the rear of Annandale House, known as Nos 1 to 4 Edis' Passage, and occupied by Messrs G. Underwood, G. Roch, William Sharp and Charles Johnson, was purchased by George Underwood for £310.

Six cottages, Nos 49 and 51, Park Street and Nos 1, 3, 5 and 7, St Catherine Street, situated at the junction of the two streets, were secured by Mr Dandoe for £430. The properties were offered upon the instructions of the trustees of the late Mr Thomas Edis. (*The Citizen*)

November 25th

1761: King George III married Princess Charlotte Sophia of Mecklenburg-Strelitz in 1761, and an association was established in honour of the occasion, which gave marriage portions to 'Young Women of Virtuous Characters', to enable them to find husbands. In Gloucester, the 'Lady Trustees' of the charity held their third meeting on this day.

Seven candidates had applied, but there were only five marriage portions remaining to be distributed. The Ladies ordered seven tickets to be made out, two of which were blanks, and then called upon each candidate, or her representative, to draw out a ticket. Those who drew prizes were entitled to £5 each, on production of their marriage certificates. Each of them would receive another £5 twelve months after they married, provided their conduct and behaviour was such as to deserve encouragement. The unlucky two who drew out blanks were assured that they would be given portions if any money remained from the present funds, or if any future legacy or benefaction should be left to the disposal of the Society. (*Bath Chronicle*)

———— ◆ ————

1874: New docks opened at Sharpness to accommodate the larger ships in use by then, which could not get up the canal to Gloucester. The opening of docks at Sharpness led to a decline in the amount of cargo which was handled at Gloucester Docks. Eventually, customs administration was moved from Gloucester to Sharpness. (Conway-Jones, H., *Gloucester Docks: An Historical Guide*, 2009)

NOVEMBER 26TH

1895: For about eight years, Gloucester had not been enforcing the law which required children to be vaccinated against smallpox. At a meeting of the Board of Guardians on this day, a letter was read out from Dr Campbell, the Medical Officer of Health for the city, reporting that there were eight cases of smallpox in the isolation hospital and that it was urgent that unprotected children were vaccinated. The Board decided that no action should be taken. Later the same day, the matter was raised again at a meeting of the Town Council, and a debate ensued as to what should be done. It was decided to do nothing.

A letter published in *The Citizen* on the next day reflected the opinion of an influential body in the city who were vehemently against vaccination. George Newman of Sutton House, Gloucester, believed that vaccinating caused more cases of smallpox than it prevented, because it gave the recipient a modified version of the illness, which turned into a full-scale version when the conditions were right. A more unusual belief of Mr Newman was that the best way of preventing or curing smallpox was to eat apples.

The decision of the Gloucester officials to do nothing resulted in an epidemic, which lasted until August the following year. By then, about 20,000 Gloucester citizens had been vaccinated, and another 5,000 re-vaccinated. (*The Citizen*)

NOVEMBER 27TH

1903: At the City Petty Sessions, Ralph McKee, a boy of 9, was charged with stealing a purse and 25s 7d on November 24th, from a jacket hanging in the Guildhall. Miss Frances Brancher, who was on a visit at Matson Rectory, had attended a bazaar at the Guildhall. While there, she took some coppers out of her purse and replaced it in the pocket of her coat, which she placed on the back of a chair. Afterwards, she realised that her purse was missing.

John McKee, the defendant's elder brother, stated that Ralph showed him the purse and said he had taken it from a lady's jacket at the Guildhall. They divided the money in Brunswick Road and threw the purse onto a shop roof in Eastgate Street.

Ralph McKee pleaded guilty to the charge. The Revd Canon Bazeley, on behalf of Miss Brancher, said she did not want any criminal punishment inflicted on the boy, but hoped he might be removed from his present surroundings to a reformatory. The Clerk said he had no authority to order that, and McKee was ordered to receive six strokes of the birch. (*The Citizen*)

NOVEMBER 28TH

1785: At about ten o'clock in the morning, the city was hit by the most violent hurricane ever remembered. It lasted about twelve to fifteen minutes, and some workmen who were repairing the Cathedral roof had to secure themselves inside the recesses of the tower. The men later declared that the whole fabric was vibrating and that they had expected the entire tower to topple down at any moment. Fortunately, only part of the battlements fell, and it was suggested that the whole thing didn't collapse because of the iron bars which perforated the stones and held the structure together. (*Gloucester Journal*)

———◆———

1899: One of the largest audiences ever seen at a school concert assembled at Shire Hall for a show given by the British Schoolchildren. Every available seat in the hall was taken, and people were even standing at the back. The first part of the show consisted of a humorous cantata called *Inspector for an Hour*, which dealt with a visit from an Education Department Inspector. The second part was taken up by some action songs and tableaux by different sections of chorus, plus a duet and a solo song. Every item met with enthusiastic applause. (*The Citizen*)

NOVEMBER 29TH

1889: On this Friday evening, a meeting of the dockers took place at the Bull Inn. The men had gone on strike that day, after a dispute had arisen at Sharpness, where the Norwegian barque *Pacific* was about to be unloaded by the lightermen, when they discovered that the cargo was to be handed out to them by foreigners. The lightermen refused to work with the Norwegians, and the masters then ordered the foreign crew to do all the work themselves.

There had been previous disputes at Bristol and Sharpness about the employment of foreigners for discharging cargoes. The men in both places had gone out on strike because of this latest incident, and the London Executive of the Bristol Dockers and General Labourers' Union had instructed its members in Gloucester to walk out in support. Mr Cook, Secretary of the Gloucester branch, asked the men to stand by him, refrain from intimidation, and behave in an orderly manner. They should go quietly home. It was agreed that a deputation would be sent to meet the masters on the next day. The dockers eventually returned to work on December 9th. (*The Citizen*)

NOVEMBER 30TH

1936: The Duchess of Beaufort opened a County Dairy School in Barrack Square. The new building was designed by the county architect, Mr R.S. Phillips. It contained an up-to-date dairy which was well-equipped with modern apparatus. There was also a lecture room, a principal's office, a cheese store and a cloakroom. The boiler houses had been fitted so as to give an abundant supply of steam for heating water and sterilizing equipment. The Duchess unlocked the door at three o'clock in the afternoon, declaring the building open. Later, in the Council Chamber at Shire Hall, she distributed prizes won by Gloucestershire dairy students during the past year. For the third time in the last five years, a cheese made by Gloucestershire students had won the Inter-County John Benson Challenge. It was reported that places at the school were already fully booked for the next two years. (*Western Daily Press*)

DECEMBER 1ST

1783: The *Gloucester Journal* commented on the dangerous overcrowding at the County Prison, in the Castle. Thirteen more miscreants had been admitted during the past week, for crimes including horse-stealing, burglary, theft and disorderly behaviour. The jail was so crowded with desperate men that the Keeper of the Prison was in great danger every night from the actions such a set of villains might be contemplating in order to escape. As a consequence, the bell, which used to be rung to summon the prisoners to prayer, had been placed on top of the Keeper's house, so that it could be used to raise the alarm in the city, if the need presented itself. (*Gloucester Journal*)

1927: A middle-aged man was taken to Gloucestershire Royal Infirmary in the afternoon, having swallowed parts of a knife, fork and spoon. He was operated upon straight away and the items of cutlery were successfully removed. He appeared to be making a good recovery. (*The Citizen*)

December 2nd

1881: Mr Dutton, lessee of the Theatre Royal in Gloucester, applied to city magistrates for a summons against a man named Sullivan for smoking in the theatre the previous night, contrary to the rules. He stated that copies of the rules were posted in different parts of the building.

The Mayor said he saw that there were regulations in force as to the proper conduct of the theatre, but it was questionable whether those regulations would enable the magistrates to grant a summons. The magistrates' clerk told Mr Dutton he would be entitled to turn out a person breaking the rules and, if necessary, to call in the assistance of the police. Mr Dutton said it was difficult to turn a man out. The Mayor said that if Mr Dutton would talk with Mr Chipp, the Deputy Chief Constable, no doubt he would put a policeman specially on duty, to render assistance if called for. Mr Nicks, one of the magistrates, commented that smoking in the theatre was exceedingly objectionable, and he was sure Mr Chipp would offer any assistance in his power.

DCC Chipp said if Mr Dutton made the usual application, a policeman would be sent. The Mayor thought the magistrates could not grant a summons in this case. Mr Nicks observed that he should be sorry for any man who smoked in the theatre after this. (*The Citizen*)

DECEMBER 3RD

1906: Gloucester Choral Society performed Elgar's *The Dream of Gerontius* at the Shire Hall. The work had been performed first at the Birmingham Festival in 1900, but it had not been played at Gloucester Cathedral as part of the Three Choirs Festival, and it seemed unlikely that it ever would be, given its subject matter, based on the poem by Cardinal Newman, concerning the subject's journey through Pergatory. Gerontius was played by Gervase Elwes, who had played the part several times before and was to become famous in the role. The Angel was played by Winifred Ludlam.

Also performed as an opener was a short work, *The Hymn of Faith*, which had been written for the last Worcester festival by Ivor Atkins. The composer conducted the choir himself. It was reported that the house was nearly full and the audience was 'thoroughly interested' by both of these modern works. (*The Citizen*)

DECEMBER 4TH

1890: Two sudden deaths occurred in Gloucester on this night. The first unfortunate was James Hooper, aged 37, who was at a smoking concert held in the club room at the Duke of Wellington Inn in Tredworth. Late in the evening, Hooper left the room and somehow missed his footing and fell down twelve stairs. Two of his friends picked him up in an unconscious state and took him to his home in Melbourne Street. A doctor was called, who pronounced Hooper dead, and said he believed he had already been dead when he was picked up in the Inn.

The second incident involved Mr Henry George Johns, who, with his father and brothers, carried on a business as ship chandlers in Commercial Road. He was a prominent member of the Northgate Wesleyan Chapel, and had gone to Quedgeley on his tricycle to conduct a Band of Hope meeting. He returned home at about nine o'clock and went to bed feeling perfectly well. About two hours later, his wife noticed that he was breathing very hard. She spoke to him but received no reply, so she fetched a doctor. Mr Johns never spoke again and died at about a quarter past twelve. He was 40 years old. (*The Citizen*)

DECEMBER 5TH

1885: The Gloucester Gordon League was launched with the opening of a new Gordon Boy's club in New Street. The national movement of the Gordon League had been started up after the death of General Charles Gordon in Khartoum, to perpetuate his memory and continue his example of working with the poor. The Gloucester branch had been set up at a meeting held in November, instigated by Mr J. Edwards, with a view to encouraging the mental and physical improvement of working lads aged from 14 to 20.

The new home of the League was officially opened by Mrs W.E. Price. A number of boys had already joined the organisation, and a large party gathered for tea. An interesting meeting was then held, presided over by the Mayor, Trevor Powell. The Very Revd the Dean of Gloucester delivered an address upon some of the traits of Gordon's character. Some vocal and instrumental music was provided by the Revd Bowers, Mr Williams (the Cathedral organist) and some of the Cathedral choirboys. (*The Citizen*)

—————•◆•—————

1903: It was announced in the press that on this evening, a 'Penny Popular Concert' was to be held at the Working Men's Institute, in Southgate Street, opposite the Infirmary. A good programme was promised, including two comic songs, humorous duets by Harry and Arthur, and a Dialogue entitled *Mixem's Matrimonial Mart*. (*Gloucester Journal*)

DECEMBER 6TH

1882: Gloucester Ornithological (and Rabbit) Society, an organisation which kept and showed caged birds (and, for a while, rabbits) held its third annual show. It was held in the old Wesleyan Day School, and the exhibits numbered nearly twice as many as in the previous year, there being about 420 entries. The society had attracted interest from beyond Gloucester, with entries in the open classes coming from London, Pembroke, Northampton, Kent and Surrey. The best bird in show was judged to be a mule (a goldfinch crossed with a linnet). There was an increase in the number of rabbits shown this year, but there was only one exhibitor of stuffed birds. Mr J. Mountney had a collection of stuffed birds and animals, which was much admired.

A founder of the society writing in 1902 said that the Ornithological Society had been formed in Gloucester in 1880. In 1881 it became an Ornithological and Rabbit Society, but the rabbits were later dropped. The Society changed its name to the Gloucester Fanciers Society in 1901. (*The Citizen*)

DECEMBER 7TH

1912: Reverend W.H. Whalley, of Brunswick Square, Gloucester, made an appeal in the local newspapers for funds to provide a Tea for sailors and boatmen in the port on Boxing Day. A similar event had been arranged last year and had proved a success. At Christmas-time, besides the sailors who might be in the Docks, there were always a large number of boatmen from Birmingham, Worcester, Ledbury and other places, and it was to minimise the temptations of the public house that this annual Tea was given. Gifts, whether in cash or in kind, would be gratefully received by Revd Whalley. (*Cheltenham Looker-on*)

———◆———

1891: The Whistling Lady, also known as 'La Belle Siffleuse', performed at the Corn Exchange. She was an American named Mrs Shaw, who had become a celebrity through her novel act. The Gloucester audience was treated to a marvellous performance from Mrs Shaw, who could whistle good music perfectly in tune, without any facial contortions. The listeners demanded several encores.

Mrs Shaw was accompanied by Edgar Hulland on piano. She had already become a celebrity in London, and had whistled for the Princess of Wales. (*The Citizen*)

DECEMBER 8TH

1945: The first post-war house built in Gloucester by a housing association was officially opened. The property, at No. 25 Brooklands Park, Longlevens, was built under a scheme by Gloucester Garden Village Ltd. It was opened by Mr R.A. Chamberlain MP, Parliamentary Secretary to the Minister of Town and Country Planning. The first tenants were Mr and Mrs Chrisp and their school-age son, who were to move into their new home on December 12th. (*Gloucester Journal*)

———◆———

1899: The Gloucester Centre of the St John Ambulance held its sixth annual competition for the Challenge Shield, at the Public Baths. The competition was designed to maintain interest in the work of the Ambulance. Only three teams had entered this year, namely The Corporation, the Police, and St Catherine's. All of them had taken part in the competition before. The Corporation had been the winners in the previous year, and the Police had won in the two years previous to that. Although the triumphant team was able to keep the Shield for a year, it had to be won for three years in succession for it to become the property of the winners. The Corporation did not get to keep the shield in pride of place in the Council Chamber at the Guildhall for another year, as St Catherine's won. (*The Citizen*)

DECEMBER 9TH

1941: The Mayor of Gloucester, Gilbert Trevor Wellington, was summonsed to appear before the City Magistrates on this day, to answer a complaint made against him by Vincent Gilbert Haines, a member of the City Council, for an alleged assault. On the evening of October 24th, the Mayor and Mayoress were at Cathedral Gardens, where they were staying as the guests of the Archdeacon of Cheltenham and his wife, when Haines came to the door, accompanied by some council tenants, demanding to see him. Haines was the leader of the tenants' association, which had been in dispute with the council for some time over a rent issue, and he had just been served with a notice to quit his house. Haines alleged that during the argument which subsequently took place, the Mayor struck him in the face. Wellington emphatically denied this, and said he had only snatched at a megaphone which Haines was about to use, but did not touch him or the megaphone.

The case was dismissed and the Bench awarded five guineas towards the cost of the defence. It was suggested by the defence counsel that Haines should be bound over to keep the peace, but the Chairman announced that they had decided it would be best for the peace of the city if they did not insist on this being done. (*Cheltenham Chronicle*)

December 10th

1906: At the Palace Theatre, Sam Redfern, a London comedian, scored a great hit with the Gloucester audience. His songs were described as 'capital', and his five-minute lecture or few words of advice was 'simply immense and kept the place in a roar throughout'. He also had 'a few words' with the band, which was very funny. Dolly Harmer, a character comedienne, performed her Suffragette song, and her imitations were equally successful. She was one of the best items on the bill.

Silent Tait, an eccentric 'prestidigitateur', was clever and amusing, his smartest trick being 'the multiplying billiard balls'. An unusual turn was given by Austin and Cowan, Australian vocalists, who performed a mixture of grand opera and comics. *Il Travatore* as a comic duet could have been a disaster, but it went down admirably. Lugio's Serenadas performed a musical 'scena', entitled *Naples by Night*, and Perci Galino did a capital imitation of a blacksmith's forge in full swing. Finally, Kid Johnson and Maisie Pelham, American novelty artistes, did a novel turn, including some smart ball punching and a good dance. (*The Citizen*)

DECEMBER 11TH

1787: Elizabeth Matthews, late of St Catherine's parish, Gloucester, appeared before Justice of the Peace Mr Hayward, charged with picking and stealing about a peck of turnips from a field in Barton Street St Michael, the property of Edward Elton Esq., of Gloucester. (*Calendar of Summary Convictions at Petty Sessions, 1781-1837*, ed. I. Wyatt, Gloucestershire Record Series, Volume 22, 2008)

———◆———

1896: An accident befell the Bishop of Gloucester, Mr Ellicott, and his wife and daughter, as they were being driven from Gloucester to the suburbs in a carriage and pair. Their carriage collided with a doctor's brougham, and the horses took fright and dashed away. Eventually the carriage was overturned and Mrs Ellicott and Miss Ellicott were thrown out. Their injuries, fortunately, did not prove to be serious, although they were badly shaken. The coachman, in his endeavours to stop the runaway horses, was dragged along for a considerable distance. (*Western Daily Press*)

DECEMBER 12TH

1990: Gloucester AFC played Cardiff City in a second round replay match in the FA Cup. Gloucester had played Dorchester at home in the first round, winning the game 2-0. Their reward was a second round game, away to Cardiff City. The game was played at Ninian Park on December 9th, and it looked for a time as if Gloucester would beat the home side, but the end result was a 2-2 draw. The replay took place at Meadow Park three days later, where dreams of progressing further in the Cup ended when Gloucester were beaten 1-0. (www.gloucestercityafc.co.uk)

DECEMBER 13TH

1766: A Special Commission of Assize was held in Gloucester to deal with a large number of rioters who were being held in the Castle gaol. In September, during severe food shortages, weavers from the Stroud Valley had marched into Gloucester to demand that farmers sell their wheat at cheaper than market value. From then on, rioting escalated in the county, with mobs visiting farms around Stroud, Cirencester and Gloucester. Prisoners were put in the county gaol to await trial, and by December there were ninety-six rioters being held there.

The next County Assizes were not due to take place until April, so an extra session of the court was needed to try some of these rioters and clear the prison. At the special commission, nine of the prisoners who had taken part in the riots were sentenced to death, and seven men were ordered to be transported. Six of the condemned men were reprieved, but the other three, Anselm Prinn, Stephen Cratchley, and Joseph Wildey, were hanged. More rioters were tried at the assizes in April, and another five of them were sentenced to be transported. (*Gloucester Journal*)

DECEMBER 14TH

1858: An inquest was held on the body of George Johns, a seaman. The captain of the *Eliza* schooner gave evidence that on the evening of Sunday, December 12th, the *Eliza*, which had a cargo of rum, was moored up in the basin against the schooner *Shamrock*. Everyone was ashore, except the captain and two masters, who were in the cabin. Hearing a noise, the captain came out of the cabin and found a man on deck who was on fire, and parts of both boats were ablaze. On the *Eliza*, it was discovered that rum was flowing out of one of the casks. Someone had bored a hole in it and a kettle containing some rum was nearby. The captain believed that the seaman from the *Shamrock* had climbed onto the *Eliza* intending to steal some rum. He bored a hole and when the rum flowed out, some got on his clothes. As it was dark and he was holding a lit candle, the flame ignited the alcohol. A verdict of accidental death was recorded. (*Gloucester Journal*)

DECEMBER 15TH

1902: Gloucester Museum was officially opened in its new home, the Price Memorial Hall building, in Brunswick Road. This building had been first opened in 1893, financed by Mrs Margaret Price as a memorial to her husband, W.E. Price, timber merchant, MP for Tewkesbury and president of the Science School. It was intended to be a lecture hall for the Art and Science Society, which was housed in the building next door, but by the time it opened, the Guildhall was being used for lectures. Eventually, it was decided to move the museum, which was housed in the building with the schools of art and science, into the Price Memorial Hall. (Rhodes, J., 'Gambier Parry and Gloucester Schools of Science and Art', in *Transactions of the Bristol and Gloucestershire Archaeological Society*, Volume 118)

DECEMBER 16TH

1820: Sir George Onesiphorus Paul died. Onesiphorus Paul was born in 1746 at Woodchester, of a family of clothiers. He added George to his name in 1780. Becoming a county magistrate in adulthood, he took a great interest in many of the public institutions of his county, and in 1780 became High Sheriff of Gloucestershire. At the Spring Assizes in 1783, when he was foreman of the Grand Jury, he addressed the jurors on the subject of the prevalence of gaol fever in the County Prison, and later published this speech. His campaigning against the conditions of the old gaol led to the building of the new county penitentiary, which opened in 1791, and several new houses of correction in various parts of the county.

Paul was buried at Woodchester. A monument was put up in Gloucester Cathedral, with an inscription which says that, thanks to Paul, the county had become 'the example and model of the best system of criminal discipline'. (*Dictionary of National Biography*; Whiting, J.R.S., *Prison Reform in Gloucestershire, 1776-1820*, 1975)

------◆------

1890: The following advertisement appeared in *The Citizen*:

Wanted, a respectable, quiet girl; one who has not been out before would suit; no Gloucester girl need apply. Address, 422, Citizen office.

DECEMBER 17TH

1918: At Shire Hall, the Duchess of Beaufort distributed a number of good service badges to a large contingent of Land Army girls, of whom there were over 350 in Gloucestershire. The Duchess said she had been so impressed with what women had accomplished on the land that she intended to take a farm herself, and with the help of Land Girls, hoped to make it pay. Lady Bledisloe, who accompanied the Duchess, had stocked a training centre for girls at Hartpury, lent for the purpose by Mrs Gordon Canning of Gloucester. (*Western Gazette*)

———— ◆ ————

1949: Television came to Gloucester on this day, when the Sutton Coldfield transmitter was switched on for public viewing. Gloucester was among the places which were able to pick up the signal. Although Gloucester was outside the radius of reception by a few miles, it was in an excellent position for reception, because the Severn Valley formed a corridor of low-lying ground from Sutton Coldfield to the city.

The opening of the transmitter was due to start at eight o'clock in the evening, but there was a short delay. When the pictures arrived, the reception of vision and sound in Gloucester proved to be very good. (*Western Daily Press*)

DECEMBER 18TH

1920: Henry William Bruton died at his home, Bewick House, in Gloucester. He had been suffering failing health for a number of years. Mr Bruton was the head of Bruton & Knowles and Co., Auctioneers and Estate Agents, who had started selling cattle at Gloucester Market fifty years previously. He had carried out a number of high profile auctions, including in May 1919, when he presided over the sale of art treasures belonging to the late Lord Redesdale of Batsford Park, where a record sum of 14,800 guineas was fetched for a portrait by Sir Joshua Reynolds.

One of the most familiar figures in Gloucester, he had been a Justice of the Peace for the city and was a prominent freemason. He was a great admirer of Charles Dickens, and owned a collection of Cruikshank sketches and cartoons. His funeral took place on December 23rd, and at his request a strictly private service was held at Matson, where he was buried. At the same time, a memorial service was held in his honour at the Cathedral. The large congregation there included the Mayor and members of the Corporation, and representatives of the many associations with which he was connected, along with a large number of friends. (*The Citizen*)

DECEMBER 19TH

1901: Archdeacon Hayward distributed prizes and addressed the scholars at the Boys' National School in London Road. Prizes were given to 152 boys, who had achieved 95 per cent or more attendances. In addition, medals were given to sixty boys who had not missed a single day of school during the year. One boy named Ashwin received a special prize for having earned the medal for five years in succession. Twenty-one others had not missed a single day's attendance for two years or more.

It had been a successful year for the school, which had earned the highest Government grant possible and had received an excellent Inspector's report. (*The Citizen*)

———◆———

1933: *The Citizen* reported that the second-class bath at the Public Baths in Barton Street had been converted into a skating rink. Boards had been put across the bath, and a gallery had been created for spectators. The rink had not been very well attended so far, but it was hoped that the public would patronise this healthy and pleasant form of winter amusement. Excellent skates were provided, and it was likely that the rink would become popular with people of all classes. (*The Citizen*)

DECEMBER 20TH

1327: According to the Parliamentary Rolls, this was the day on which King Edward II was buried in St Peter's Abbey (other sources say December 21st). The deposed king had been murdered in Berkeley Castle in September, and for a time it seemed that no-one wanted to carry out his burial, but then Abbot Thoky had the late king's body brought to Gloucester. The funeral was a proper state affair, attended by Edward's widow and his son, the new king. The details of his death were not widely known at that time. The decision to volunteer to bury Edward II proved to be a good one for Gloucester, as the King, who had been unpopular in life, came to be seen as a martyr after his death, and Gloucester became a place of pilgrimage, thus bringing a great deal of wealth into the town. (*Parliamentary Rolls of Medieval England*, ed. C. Given-Wilson et al, 2005)

DECEMBER 21ST

1943: Children living at the Homes run by the Gloucester Social Welfare Committee were given a party by Canadian airmen based in Gloucester, at the Limes. About sixty Canadians attended, and gave a concert and a picture show. They also provided a Christmas tree with presents, and each airman acted as a foster-father to a child. (*The Citizen*)

<hr>

1888: *The Citizen* included a guide to Christmas in the Gloucester shops. The city tradesmen had made extensive preparations for the festive season, and novelties and attractive articles could be seen in most of the shop windows.

Drapers in particular had stocked their establishments with the most seasonable and fashionable specialities. Mr Lance's in Westgate Street had one window devoted to evening costumes for the dancing season. Grocers were not far behind the drapers in their attractions. Southerns, of Northgate Street, had large quantities of seasonable fruits, while Sterry and Morris of Southgate Street had fruit, biscuits and provisions of all kinds. Messrs Talbot of Gloucester and Monmouth had some non-alcoholic drinks, recommended for parties and the ballroom, and Thomas and Co. were selling wines and spirits of good quality at reasonable prices. Winfield & Son of Westgate Street had evergreens, grasses, flowers and bouquets for decorations, and Mr C.H. Dancey, stationer, had tastefully hand-painted Christmas cards, and his window was artistically arranged. (*The Citizen*)

DECEMBER 22ND

1879: At the City Police Court, Mr C. Overthrow, a resident of Longsmith Street, made an application to the magistrates to be protected from a nuisance created at Wellington Hall by people calling themselves 'The Salvation Army'. For the last four Sundays he had got no rest because of the disturbances. He had even had his front door burst open by them, when they had gone outside preaching and the crowd pressed on the door, which gave way. He had put shutters up to stop his windows being broken. They started at seven in the morning and went on until ten o'clock at night.

DCC Chipp said the Army rendered the street impassable, and their conduct was outrageous. They would form themselves into a small company, four deep, and a woman walked in front giving the tune and waving her handkerchief. They paraded round the streets, and all the worst characters in Gloucester gathered round them and sang songs of their own. The Chairman told Mr Chipp to deal with the nuisance, according to his judgement.

The Salvation Army had come to Gloucester in this year, under the leadership of Pamela Shepherd. They used Wellington Hall at first, but later moved to Kings Barton Street. In 1960, they opened a new building at the corner of Barton Street and Park Street. (*The Citizen*; *A History of the County of Gloucester, Volume IV, The City of Gloucester*, ed. N.M. Herbert, 1988)

DECEMBER 23RD

1894: On this Sunday evening, two deserters from the Duke of Cornwall's Light Infantry were being escorted from Cardiff to Liverpool, en route for Ireland. They were making the journey by train, in the charge of a sergeant and a private of the regiment. Shortly before six o'clock they arrived at Gloucester, where they had to change platforms from the Great Western to the Midland. During this manouevre, the pair managed to escape. The sergeant informed the Gloucester police, who were still looking for the escapees the next day. The two prisoners were Jesse Cobb, aged 21, who was a native of Gloucester, and Francis Carne, aged 23, who was believed to be from Cheltenham. The two men were handcuffed together, but they were seen to be separated shortly after their disappearance. (*The Citizen*)

———◆———

1861: While the funeral of Prince Albert, Queen Victoria's husband, was taking place in London, a service was held in Gloucester Cathedral, at which the new Bishop of Gloucester and Bristol, Dr Thomson, preached. The Mayor and Corporation attended in State, and all business was suspended for the day. (*Western Daily Press*)

DECEMBER 24TH

1143: Milo of Gloucester died. He was the son of Walter of Gloucester, who was the County Sheriff from 1104 to 1121. Milo succeeded his father as Sheriff. In 1135, after persistent attacks by the local population, the monks of Llanthony Priory in the Black Mountains retreated to Gloucester. Milo founded Llanthony Secunda Piory in Gloucester for them, in 1136. He was in the service of Henry I from 1130 to 1135, and became Constable of England. When Henry died, his nephew Stephen declared himself king. Milo continued as Constable under him and entertained the new king at Gloucester Castle in May 1138. Stephen was opposed by Matilda, Henry's daughter, whom Milo was persuaded was the rightful claimant to the throne, and he changed his allegiance. He entertained Matilda at the castle in September 1139. In 1141, Matilda made Milo the first Earl of Hereford. He was killed while out hunting in the Forest of Dean, supposedly by accident. He was buried at Llanthony Secunda. (Langston, J.N., 'Priors of Llanthony by Gloucester', in *Transactions of the Bristol and Gloucestershire Archaeological Society*, Volume 63)

DECEMBER 25TH

1903: Christmas Day was celebrated at Gloucester Workhouse. The building had been tastefully decorated by officials and inmates, with evergreens and mottos. A service was held in the chapel in the morning, and at lunchtime 314 people sat down to a dinner of roast beef and plum pudding, with drinks of either lemonade or beer. Packets of tea, sugar and tobacco were distributed among the inmates. After dinner, the Chaplain presented each officer and inmate with a Christmas letter. The inmates were left to their own devices during the afternoon, then at tea-time, as well as the usual fare, there was a plentiful supply of cake and other good things. A special service was held in the chapel in the evening, at which carols were sung by the choir of Holy Trinity Church, Longlevens.

Presents had been sent by various companies and individuals, consisting of sweets and jam, toys, scarves, cuffs and socks, oranges and crackers, evergreens, and biscuits for the babies. The Master and Matron, Mr and Mrs Bennett, had been untiring in their efforts to make the day enjoyable for the inmates in their charge. (*The Citizen*)

DECEMBER 26TH

1814: *The Gloucester Journal* published a report with the headline, 'A WARNING TO SABBATH-BREAKERS', concerning two city boys, named Lodge and Hoskins, who had gone into the fields on a Sunday to shoot birds. As they made their way through a hedge, the muzzle of the gun of one struck the butt of his companion's piece and went off, discharging all of its contents into the sides of Lodge. He was taken to the Infirmary, where he died two days later. (*Gloucester Journal*)

———◆———

1887: A tremendous crowd gathered in the Royal Albert Theatre for the first performance of the pantomime, *Cinderella*. Previous pantomimes had come to Gloucester after appearing for the Christmas season at Worcester, so generally the cast and scenery were pretty tired by then, and it started too late in the season. This year, Val Simpson had produced a pantomime especially for Gloucester. The press reporter who witnessed the first performance believed that pantomime these days was 'really only a variety entertainment disguised under the barest outline of a plot and full of stupid jokes and the vilest puns', and *Cinderella* was no exception to this general rule. The audience, though, enjoyed it. The panto included the usual topical songs, and there were local allusions to the Gas Works, the Baths, the Town Council, etc. No one in the Boxing night audience could complain that they had not had their money's worth. (*The Citizen*)

DECEMBER 27TH

1803: Thomas Stock, co-founder with Robert Raikes of the Gloucester Sunday School movement, died. Born in Gloucester in 1749, the son of a Gloucester freeman, he attended the King's School from 1757. After being ordained, he went as curate to Ashbury in Berkshire, where, in 1777, he set up a Sunday school in the church nave. Later, he returned to Gloucester and became master of St Catherine's Parish Grammar School and Curate of St John's Church, Northgate Street. In around 1779, he became Headmaster of King's School, and in 1787 he became perpetual curate of St Aldates. With surgeon Charles Brandon Tryme, he founded a laying-in charity in Gloucester for poor women. He started the Sunday school in Gloucester with Robert Raikes in 1780. Stock was buried at St Aldates. A memorial to him was erected in the Cathedral. (*Oxford Dictionary of National Biography*)

DECEMBER 28TH

1865: The Mayor of Gloucester gave a banquet at the Judges' Lodgings. About 120 guests attended, including the Recorder, the Bishop, and most of the magistrates. The bill of fare consisted of: eight tureens of turtle soup, one tureen of soup *Julienne*; three turbots, three cod, four dishes of stewed lamperns; two dishes of sweetbreads, volauvents *a la Financiere*; four dishes of mutton cutlets, four dishes of oyster patties; a hind quarter of lamb, four haunches of mutton, two pieces of roast beef, two stewed rumps of beef; four turkeys bechamel, two couples brace pheasants, two brace of wild ducks; four Boudings, *Glaces a la compte de Nesselrode*, four cabinet puddings, four plum puddings, six dishes of mince pies, six moulds of jellies and creams, strawberry and *millo-fruit* ices. This was followed by dessert. (*Western Daily Press*)

December 29th

1941: Gloucester Post Office Orchestra gave a concert of light music at the Guildhall, under the auspices of the Gloucester War Charities Association. This was their first appearance as a concert orchestra. At the time, this was the only Post Office orchestra in the country. (*Gloucester Journal*)

1856: There had been agitation throughout the country caused by the belief that the government was going to extend the payment of 16 pence in the pound income tax, as it was supposed to have been a temporary measure to finance the Crimean War, which had ended in March. In Gloucester, a meeting was held on this day, at which Mr S. Bowley and Mr T.M. Sturge spoke in favour of a resolution which condemned the tax as 'unjust in its application, oppressive in its execution, vexatious in its assessments, and demoralizing in its tendancy'. Admiral Sir M.F.F. Berkeley came forward to say a few words in opposition to the resolution. He didn't agree that the tax should be abolished straight away, as the money was needed to keep up the army and navy, which upheld Britain's high standing in the world. Britain also needed to pay her debts. A majority were in favour of sending a petition to Parliament, embodying the views of the meeting in opposition to the income tax. (*Bristol Mercury*)

DECEMBER 30TH

1935: A man had to be rescued from his bathroom at No.184 Calton Road. Frederick Cartwright, aged 62, had turned on the water and geyser in his bathroom to fill the bath. Somehow, after turning off the water and putting out the gas, he accidentally turned the gas on again, without noticing. He had shut the window and locked the door before getting into the tub. When he realised that something was wrong, he got out and fell onto the floor. Downstairs, his wife and daughter heard him fall. When he didn't answer their calls, they fetched a neighbour, who smashed the bathroom door in with an axe and found Mr Cartwright unconscious on the floor. He was taken to Gloucester Royal Infirmary, but regained consciousness before he got there. (*Cheltenham Chronicle*)

DECEMBER 31ST

1909: Every year from 1884, two Christmas dinners for poor elderly folk had been given by John Ward, a local councillor, and the tradition was continued by the terms of his will after he died in 1895. On this occasion, the guests were entertained by a new vocal group called the 'Gloucester Civic Vocal Quartette'. The group was made up of the Mayor, Ald F. Hannam-Clark (bass), the Mayoress, Mrs Hannam-Clark (contralto), the City High Sheriff, Dr E. Dykes-Bower (tenor); and Mrs Dykes-Bower (soprano). The group performed at this first dinner, and would also be at the second one, to be held on January 3rd 1910. They had already performed at previous charity events, and were available to carry out other engagements. (*Who's Who in Gloucester*, 1910)

———◆———

1942: Wartime anxieties were put aside for one night as the citizens of Gloucester celebrated the end of the old year and saw in the new one. People seemed determined to enjoy themselves, as the demand for tickets to dances had exceeded supply, and there were many parties. In most cases, the entertainments concluded half an hour before midnight, and many of the dancers then joined the crowds at the Cross, where, as the clock struck midnight, hundreds joined hands and sang *Auld Lang Syne*. (*The Citizen*)